CW00829285

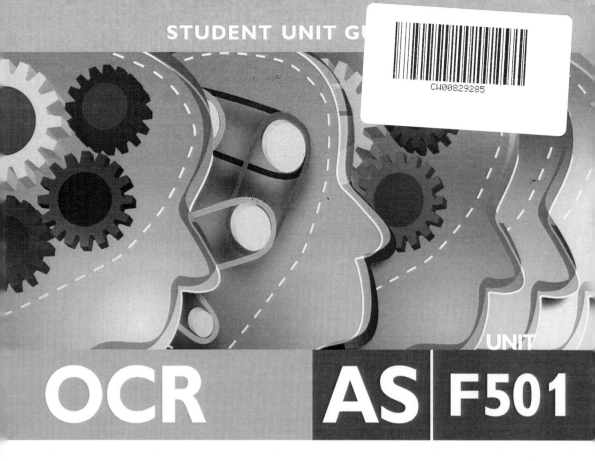

# OCR

## AS | F501

UNIT

# Critical Thinking

Introduction to Critical Thinking

Roy van den Brink-Budgen

Philip Allan Updates, an imprint of Hodder Education, an Hachette UK company, Market Place, Deddington, Oxfordshire, OX15 0SE

**Orders**

Bookpoint Ltd, 130 Milton Park, Abingdon, Oxfordshire, OX14 4SB
tel: 01235 827827
fax: 01235 400401
e-mail: education@bookpoint.co.uk
Lines are open 9.00 a.m.–5.00 p.m., Monday to Saturday, with a 24-hour message answering service. You can also order through the Philip Allan Updates website: www.philipallan.co.uk

© Philip Allan Updates 2009

ISBN 978-0-340-96934-2

First printed 2009
Impression number 5 4
Year 2014 2013

This guide has been written specifically to support students preparing for the OCR AS Critical Thinking Unit F501 examination. The content has been neither approved nor endorsed by OCR and remains the sole responsibility of the author.

Typeset by Phoenix Photosetting, Chatham, Kent
Printed by CPI Group (UK) Ltd, Croydon CR0 4YY

Hachette UK's policy is to use papers that are natural, renewable and recyclable products and made from wood grown in sustainable forests. The logging and manufacturing processes are expected to conform to the environmental regulations of the country of origin.

P01597

# Contents

## Introduction

■ ■ ■

## Content Guidance

■ ■ ■

## Questions and Answers

# Introduction

## About this guide

This guide looks in detail at what is needed for good performance in the OCR AS F501 paper (Unit 1): Introduction to Critical Thinking. It does this by considering the skills required and exploring how these skills are assessed by the sort of questions that you will find in this paper.

In the Content Guidance section all the skills are explained, demonstrated, and illustrated with examples.

In the Questions and Answers section you'll find these skills applied to sample exam questions. Sample answers are given — the good, the mediocre and the bad — with explanations of how an examiner would assess them.

## Skills

Critical thinking is primarily concerned with how claims are used as the basis for argument and other claims, known as inferences, are drawn from them. These claims and inferences are normally referred to as *arguments*.

Unit F501 is concerned with the analysis and evaluation of such arguments. To do well in this unit, you therefore need the skills to analyse arguments and to evaluate both claims and arguments.

What exactly are these skills?
- analysing the (explicit) structure of arguments
- identifying assumptions
- evaluating evidence used in arguments
- evaluating reasoning of arguments
- understanding what are called *credibility criteria*
- applying credibility criteria to claims

In addition to having these skills of analysis and evaluation, you will also need to be able to write a *reasoned case*. This involves coming to a judgement between opposing positions by reasoning. In other words, you're being asked to write an *argument*. So the final skill is:
- writing a reasoned case (an argument) in support of a judgement

As with any set of skills (like those needed for swimming or playing a musical instrument), if you've got them and you've practised them enough, you should be at least reasonably competent. So keep this list of skills close by you. Tick off the skills you already have. Mark those that you're not so strong in, including those which you need to practise more.

# The examiner and the mark scheme

While you should have a reasonable level of competence if you've got the skills and you've practised them sufficiently, does this mean that the route to success in Unit F501 is now fully open?

Perhaps not: as well as having the skills, you need to understand what the examiner is looking for. So this book will help you to see how to keep an examiner happy.

Examiners will mark your examination papers according to an agreed mark scheme. For some questions there will be only one way to get full marks. With some other questions, however, the range of correct answers can be much broader. In these cases, when examiners come across alternative correct answers and unexpected approaches they will give marks that fairly reflect the relevant knowledge and skills demonstrated. This applies, for example, when you're asked for additional reasons to support a position. So where does our examiner draw the line in a question like this? At the point where the additional reason is not relevant or plausible.

# The examination

Let's just remind ourselves what the paper looks like. You'll be given a resource booklet containing various documents. These will include different types of evidence (including statistical evidence) and could also include a visual image. Any information that you are not expected to know already will be explained.

The question paper will be divided into two sections. They are of almost equal importance in terms of the number of marks available.

## Section A

Section A consists of questions testing your analysis and evaluation skills. It provides 35 of the 75 marks.

It will include questions such as these:
- State the main conclusion of the argument in paragraphs $x$ and $y$.
- Identify the reasons that support the main conclusion in paragraphs $x$ and $y$.
- Identify the counter-argument in paragraphs $x$ and $y$.
- What argument component (or 'element') is the following?
- State the assumption that is being made by the author when they make claim $x$.
- State one example that is used to support the argument in Document 1.
- Explain why the evidence used in paragraph $x$ might or might not be representative.
- Explain one way in which the image/photograph of $x$ might give support to the caption that is below it.
- Suggest an additional reason to support...

- Evaluate the argument given in paragraph $z$ by assessing the extent to which the reasons support the conclusion.

## Section B

Section B provides the other 40 of the 75 marks. The questions in this section will all be concerned with applying credibility criteria to the documents in the resource booklet. Questions could include the following:

- Assess how far the report in Document 1 is credible. In doing this, you should make two points. In each case you should identify and use a relevant credibility criterion to assess credibility.
- Assess the credibility of a claim made by $X$ and one made by $Y$. Apply credibility criteria to explain how these might strengthen or weaken the credibility of these claims.
- Explain what further information is needed to support your assessment of the credibility of the claim made by $X$.
- In what way might a claim made within Document 2 be consistent with a claim made by $X$?
- In what way might a claim made within Document 2 be inconsistent with a claim made by $X$?
- Referring to the material within the documents, come to a reasoned judgement as to... You should make a reasoned case, with a judgement based on the relative credibility of both sides and the relative plausibility of both positions.

# Revision

For most of your subjects, you'll be encouraged to work out a scheme for revising the material that you need for the exam, so that by the time you do the exam you'll know enough to deal with the questions.

Critical thinking isn't like that. There isn't much you can do to revise. The main thing is to check that you're familiar with the few technical terms that are used. These are listed at the end of the Content Guidance section.

Critical thinking is essentially a set of skills, and since we get more skilful at something the more we practise it (think of music, dancing, juggling and so on), the best preparation for the exam is to do a lot of practising. You should look at arguments, good, bad or indifferent. You should look specifically at how evidence has been used in these arguments.

# Content Guidance

**U**nit F501 assesses the three main skill areas of critical thinking. These are analysis, evaluation, and production of argument.

The paper is divided into two parts, of almost equal value in terms of marks. The first part of the paper, Section A, provides 35 of the 75 marks and is concerned with analysis and evaluation of argument. The second part, Section B, provides the other 40 marks and is concerned with credibility issues: you have to apply various credibility criteria to material in order to assess how credible it is. These credibility issues fit into the skills of evaluation, which means that these evaluation skills are by far the most important for the Unit F501 paper. Skills in producing argument are required only in the final question of the paper.

In this Content Guidance section we start with analysis for two reasons. First, because the first few questions that you'll do on the paper are analysis questions. Second (and more important) is that if you haven't got some skills in analysis, you can't get very far with evaluation.

# Analysis of arguments

## Skills and terms

What skills are we looking at here?

- the ability to distinguish between the different parts of an argument: reasons and conclusions
- the ability to identify counter-claims/counter-assertions and counter-arguments
- the ability to identify counter-arguments and the conclusions and reason(s) in them
- the ability to identify the place of evidence (including examples) in reasoning
- the ability to identify hypothetical reasoning
- the ability to state assumptions that are made

You will notice that OCR sometimes uses the term *argument element* for what it also calls *argument component*. These components are also given the familiar terms *reason*, *conclusion*, *hypothetical reasoning* and *counter-claim/counter-assertion/counter-argument*. Although the term *argument component* is more widely used for parts of an argument, we'll use *argument element* when we are looking at sample questions.

## Reasons and conclusions

We'll start with some basic analysis, looking at very simple arguments.

> Children today have much more money than those of 50 years ago. So children live very different lives to those of 50 years ago.
>
> Children have much more leisure than those of 50 years ago. So children live very different lives to those of 50 years ago.
>
> There are many more technological goods available for children today compared with 50 years ago (computers, mobile phones, and so on). So children live very different lives to those of 50 years ago.

It should be very clear what's going on in each of these. In each case, there is one **reason** (R) which is used to draw one **conclusion** (C).

R

C

In each case, there is no more than this going on. And as you can see, the conclusion is the same in each argument. This shows us that we could combine these three arguments into one:

> Children today have much more money than those of 50 years ago. Children have much more leisure than those of 50 years ago. There are many more technological goods available for children today compared with 50 years ago (computers, mobile phones, and so on). So children live very different lives to those of 50 years ago.

Now we have the following structure:

R1  R2  R3
↘   ↓   ↙
C

The structure remains the same, whichever way we organise the argument.

> Children live very different lives to those of 50 years ago. This is because of three changes in the lives of children. Children today have much more money than those of 50 years ago. Children have much more leisure than those of 50 years ago. There are many more technological goods available for children today compared with 50 years ago (computers, mobile phones, and so on).

We've now got the conclusion at the beginning and we've added a connecting sentence, but the actual argument remains the same. This is one of the things that you're asked to do: work out what the argument is.

## The main conclusion: 'What's going on?'

Although you're asked to find the main conclusion and reasons in an argument, this is like being asked the simple question, 'What's going on?' This question, as we'll see, is a very useful way to focus our thinking.

It's like when you see something happening in the street. For example, there's a scuffle or someone's running away from a shop and being chased by other people. If you're asked, 'What's going on?' you don't give all the detail about what everybody was doing ('There's someone there with a red top who's eating a chocolate bar'). Instead you describe the main action with enough detail as is necessary to do this.

So when we ask, 'What's going on?' in the argument above, you know that the simple answer is, 'The author is saying/arguing that "children live very different lives to those of 50 years ago".'

As you can see, then, a simple way of getting to the main conclusion of any argument is to ask and then answer the question, 'What's going on?'

Let's try it with a longer argument:

> Though gambling companies can now advertise more widely, there are restrictions on how they can do this. These include no television advertising before the 9 p.m. watershed. Another is that, if a football club is sponsored by

> a gambling company, the company logo should not feature on the children's replica football shirt. This is in order to stop children being involved in advertising gambling. However, restricting the involvement of children will not necessarily work. Companies might be less willing to sponsor a club (or be less willing to pay so much) if their logo can't be used on all the club's merchandise. The online casino Mansion pays over £30 million to have its logo on all Tottenham shirts, including children's shirts. In addition, many older children need to have the larger shirts, so will have to wear adult shirts.

This is a much busier argument, with a lot more happening. Before we have a look at the detail, we'll ask the question: 'What's going on?'

You will probably have seen what's going on: the author is arguing that trying to prevent children being involved in advertising of gambling won't necessarily work. This claim sits right in the middle of the passage. How did we get to see this?

Because when we ask what's going on in the passage, we can see how it is divided up. It opens up for us:

> Though gambling companies can now advertise more widely, there are restrictions on how they can do this. These include no television advertising before the 9 p.m. watershed. *[This is background information, some of which doesn't play any further part in the argument.]*
>
> Another is that, if a football club is sponsored by a gambling company, the company logo should not feature on the children's replica football shirt. This is in order to stop children being involved in advertising gambling. *[This is leading us, as we subsequently see, in the main direction of the argument.]*
>
> However, restricting the involvement of children will not necessarily work. *[And here is what the argument is about. Even a quick scan through the rest of it is enough to confirm this.]*
>
> Companies might be less willing to sponsor a club (or be less willing to pay so much) if their logo can't be used on all the club's merchandise. The online casino Mansion pays over £30 million to have its logo on all Tottenham shirts, including children's shirts. In addition, many older children need to have the larger shirts, so will have to wear adult shirts. *[Here we have the reasons for the conclusion — two of them.]*

### The 'however' test

What we have seen is that the 'What's going on?' method gets us to the conclusion pretty quickly. You can sometimes check for conclusions by looking for particular words (such as *so*, *therefore*, and *thus*), but this method wouldn't have helped you here. In fact, it would have led you astray by taking you to the second half of the last sentence.

What is significant, though, is the use of the word *however*. This can often highlight that something important is going on in an argument. It's very often used to signal that an author's argument is about to begin. And this example fits with that.

The 'however' test is a useful guide to looking quickly at an argument, although it's not normally given to you. You can see how it would be useful. The use of the word *however* (or alternatives such as *but* or *on the other hand*) indicates a shift in direction, and this shift is normally in the direction of the author's argument, after he or she has referred to a different position.

### The 'therefore' test

You're also sometimes asked to use the 'therefore' test. In this test you put the word *therefore* in front of a statement to see if it works as a conclusion. Though this can be useful, you'd have probably already worked out the conclusion using the 'What's going on?' method long before you returned to the statement 'restricting the involvement of children will not necessarily work' to use the 'therefore' test.

## The reasons

We've described a useful way of quickly finding the main conclusion. There is a similarly quick way to find the reasons. Having found out what's going on, you are now looking for why the author thinks this. In other words,

**What's going on? *X* is going on.**

**Why does the author think *X*? Because of this (and that and...)**

### Content and sequence

Another clue to look for is content and sequence. If there is more than one reason (and in the questions you're dealing with there will be), then you're looking for separate chunks of content. Look again at the reasons in the above argument.

> Companies might be less willing to sponsor a club (or be less willing to pay so much) if their logo can't be used on all the club's merchandise. *[Here's one chunk of content.]*
>
> Many older children need to have the larger shirts, so will have to wear adult shirts. *[Here's another.]*

So two chunks of content following each other looked very much like reasons.

### Examples and evidence

What about the missing sentence?

> The online casino Mansion pays over £30 million to have its logo on all Tottenham shirts, including children's shirts.

This sentence is an **example** which develops the reason that came before it. Examples are a type of **evidence**. They're used when the author wants to illustrate a reason in order to give emphasis to what's being argued. It's a familiar way of arguing. So what's the difference between examples and evidence? We've already stated that examples are a type of evidence, so we've established that the two are not distinct categories.

What's happening in this claim?

> The average British woman will vacuum a distance of 7,300 miles in her life-time; men will vacuum only 850 miles.

Do we have one or two examples? Do we have evidence?

Is this an example of the difference between British men and women in terms of house-work done? In terms of the different roles of men and women? Are there two examples: one of women and one of men? Is this evidence relating to the different roles/tasks of women and men?

It would not be inaccurate to say 'yes' to all these questions. As we can see, the information is both example and evidence.

We can't say that size distinguishes between example and evidence. It could well be that the information on vacuuming has been drawn from a survey involving thousands of people. Where we can make progress in making a distinction is when the author cites an example illustrating a piece of evidence they've just given.

> People who play violent computer games must be affected negatively by what they see on the screen in front of them. Studies have shown that people who play violent computer games like *Grand Theft Auto IV* can be more aggressive after they've played the games. A taxi driver was murdered in Thailand by a young man who claimed that he was trying to recreate a scene from *Grand Theft Auto IV*. Thus we should ask gaming companies to reduce the violent content of the games they produce.

In this argument, the author gives a reason (first sentence) and supports it with evidence (second sentence) illustrated by an example (third sentence) in order to draw the conclusion (last sentence).

This argument shows how an example can illustrate evidence. It also shows how a reason can be supported by evidence. So if we were to depict the structure of the argument, it would be simple:

$$R$$
$$\downarrow$$
$$C$$

We could depict it in a more detailed way to show the evidence and the example:

$$R \ (+ \ Ev_{ \ + \ Ex})$$
$$\downarrow$$
$$C$$

As you can see, we've shown the example as less significant than the evidence, which reflects how it is used in the argument. We've also shown both the evidence and the example in brackets, to show that they are not a necessary part of the *structure* of the argument, although they are part of its content.

### Reasons, evidence and example

So how do we distinguish between reasons on the one hand and evidence and examples on the other? In the argument we've just looked at, both the evidence and the example developed the reason that came before them. They are neither additional reasons nor part of the reason. If they weren't there, the argument could still proceed. This is the best way to look at it. If evidence or examples weren't there, could the argument still stand *in the same way*? In this case, it could. This is the most effective test. But remember that the words *in the same way* are very important. It's not just whether the argument could still stand, but whether it could stand with the same reasons.

To put it very simply, then, the key to understanding the difference between reasons on the one hand and evidence and examples on the other is how the latter are used.

When answering questions that ask you for the reasons the author uses, you will see that you need to be careful in giving *only* the actual reason(s) without any additional evidence and/or examples.

# Counter-assertions and counter-arguments

You'll remember that we were looking above at the likely significance in an argument of words like *however* and *but*. We saw that they often indicated that the author was starting their own argument, having presented a different position.

In such cases the author may be presenting a **counter-assertion** (often referred to as a **counter-claim**) or **counter-argument**. The word 'counter' tells us that it's an opposing position. The difference between a counter-assertion or counter-claim and a counter-argument is simple. A counter-argument, as an argument, includes at least one reason leading to at least one conclusion. A counter-assertion/counter-claim is simply a statement that opposes the author's argument.

## Counter-arguments

Look at the next argument. Remember to ask yourself, 'What's going on?'

> It is often argued that people should walk or cycle to work or school rather than use a car. This is because, it is claimed, using a car contributes much more to global warming. However, the production of food requires so much energy that far more carbon is emitted in providing a person with enough calories to walk than would be emitted by using a car. Thus the climate would benefit if we exercised less and drove more.

By now you're sufficiently tuned in to how asking this question takes you to the conclusion. We can see that in the end the author is telling us that 'the climate would benefit if we exercised less and drove more'. You'll also have spotted that there's one reason given in support of this conclusion. And, hopefully, you'll have seen the significance of the word *however*. In this argument it signalled a shift away from an opposing position. And this opposing position is in the form of an argument.

> Using a car rather than walking contributes much more to global warming. Therefore people should walk or cycle to work or school rather than use a car.

This, then, is a counter-argument. We've repackaged it here to emphasise the form of the argument, but you could have used your 'What's going on?' question to work out the reason and the conclusion.

## Counter-assertion

What about the next version?

> It is often argued that for the sake of the environment, people should walk or cycle to work or school rather than use a car. However, the production of food requires so much energy that far more carbon is emitted in providing a person with enough calories to walk than would be emitted by using a car. Thus the climate would benefit if we exercised less and drove more.

In this version, though the author refers to an argument ('It is often argued that...'), they don't present their information in the form of one. In this example, then, the counter-position is given in the form of a **counter-assertion**.

## Hypothetical reasoning

In the next version of this argument, something else is happening.

> According to Green Party representative Chris Goodall, driving a typical car for 3 miles adds about 0.9 kg of carbon dioxide to the atmosphere. On the other hand, walking 3 miles will typically use about 180 calories. To replace these calories would require about 100 g of beef. Given that the production of beef requires so much energy, 100 g of beef results in 3.6 kg of emissions (four times the amount for taking the car). Therefore, if people reduced their levels of exercise and thus ate less, then global warming would be reduced. It is obvious that we should do both of these things.

Hopefully you will have spotted that the last but one sentence is in the form of *if...then...* This is normally referred to as **hypothetical reasoning**. We can have hypothetical conclusions and hypothetical arguments. They all share the same characteristic of the *if...then...* form or an equivalent ('Supposing that...then...', and so on) or its reversed form ('This will follow if that is done').

What about the next argument?

> It is important for people to realise what effects they will have on the environment if they eat beef and other meat. People should worry much more about this than about whether or not their television is on standby and what sort of light bulbs they're using. A public education campaign should be created which brings home to people what they're doing when they next tuck in to a beefburger.

In this example, the conclusion (which hopefully you found by asking, 'What's going on?') is drawn from the previous reasoning about the effects on the environment of meat-eating. But is there hypothetical reasoning going on? Obviously there's an 'if' there, so does it indicate something hypothetical?

Look at the relevant sentence carefully.

> It is important for people to realise what effects they will have on the environment if they eat beef and other meat.

In this example the hypothetical is still there but needs a little unpacking. What's going on here is this:

> It is important for people to realise that if they eat beef and other meat, then there will be effects on the environment.

If the examination asks you to say what a certain part of an argument is, and it's hypothetical reasoning, then that's obviously what you write. You might also be asked to explain why you have given this answer. This does seem rather odd. Question: Why have you identified that part of the argument as hypothetical reasoning? Answer: Because it uses the form of hypothetical reasoning! It's all very circular. So how are you supposed to answer this question?

Let's do this using the hypothetical element in an earlier argument.

> Therefore if people reduced their levels of exercise and thus ate less, then global warming would be reduced. It is obvious that we should do both of these things.

Why, then, are we describing this as hypothetical reasoning? What is the examiner looking for? The following should do it:

**It is a reason that consists of a condition (people reducing their levels of exercise and thus eating less) being necessary for a consequence (the reduction of global warming) to follow.**

# Assumptions

We've now covered the following skills of analysis:

- the ability to distinguish between the different parts of an argument: reasons and conclusions
- the ability to identify counter-claims/counter-assertions and counter-arguments (and the reasons and conclusions in them)
- the ability to identify evidence (including examples) in arguments
- the ability to identify hypothetical reasoning

The only one left is the skill of finding **assumptions**. Note that this is not about evaluating assumptions. Let's be clear what we mean by the term 'assumption':

**An assumption in an argument is a *reason* in that argument.**

**An assumption in an argument is an *unstated reason* in that argument.**

**An assumption in an argument is a *necessary, though unstated, reason* in that argument.**

If you say, 'The author has to assume X, but there's a problem with assuming this because...', then you're evaluating an assumption. But if you're asked to *identify* an assumption, you're not being asked to *evaluate* it. All you have to do when asked to identify an assumption is to *state* what is a reason in the argument.

So, let's find some assumptions.

You'll remember the simple arguments we looked at right at the beginning of this section.

> Children today have much more money than those of 50 years ago. So children live very different lives to those of 50 years ago.
>
> Children have much more leisure than those of 50 years ago. So children live very different lives to those of 50 years ago.
>
> There are many more technological goods available for children today compared with 50 years ago (computers, mobile phones, and so on). So children live very different lives to those of 50 years ago.

What assumptions are being made in these arguments?

> Children today have much more money than those of 50 years ago. So children live very different lives to those of 50 years ago.

You can see that here the author moves from a piece of information about children today to a *judgement* about children today. The thing that connects the two is that the author gives the information a meaning or significance. This is what is happening:

> Children today have much more money than those of 50 years ago. *[The significance of this information is 'having more money leads to children living very different lives'.]* So *[because of this information having this significance]* children live very different lives to those of 50 years ago.

You can see two things here. First, the reason that gives significance to the evidence is *not stated*. Second, this statement of significance is *necessary* in enabling the conclusion to be drawn. As a result, the statement 'having more money leads to children living very different lives' is an assumption in this argument.

## The negative test

Many years ago I devised a test to show whether a statement is assumed. This is the 'negative test'. It is very simple and always works. All we do is put the statement into its negative form and see what happens to the argument.

> Children today have much more money than those of 50 years ago. Having more money does not lead to children living very different lives. So children live very different lives to those of 50 years ago.

As you can see, this simply doesn't work. This is because it is now a plain contradiction. Since the negative version blows the argument apart, the statement we offered is clearly essential to the argument. You can try this with the other two arguments. What is the author assuming?

> Children have much more leisure than those of 50 years ago. So children live very different lives to those of 50 years ago.

> There are many more technological goods available for children today compared with 50 years ago (computers, mobile phones, and so on). So children live very different lives to those of 50 years ago.

## Identifying assumptions

Of course, arguments can (and often do) involve plenty of assumptions. The fact that they do doesn't mean that such arguments are weak. We can have arguments that are pretty strong but still contain plenty of assumptions. Some people misunderstand this. To say an argument is not very good *because* it includes a lot of assumptions shows confused thinking.

What assumptions can we find in another argument we looked at earlier?

> It is important for people to realise what effects they will have on the environment if they eat beef and other meat. People should worry much more about this than about whether or not their television is on standby and what sort of light bulbs they're using. A public education campaign should be created which brings home to people what they're doing when they next tuck in to a beefburger.

Here are some:

- Affecting the environment in negative ways is something that people should seek to reduce.
- Public education campaigns to inform people of the effects of meat-eating on the environment will get people to change their behaviour.
- People don't already know about the effects on the environment of eating meat.

You can see how each of these is necessary to connect the claim in the first sentence with the recommendation which is the conclusion.

And you can see that finding these assumptions is nothing to do with evaluating the argument!

Given that when we're looking for assumptions, we're looking for statements that the author of an argument *must* believe to be true in order to argue as they do, it is vital that we are accurate. If we're asked to give an assumption in an argument or part of an argument, then we need to ensure that we express this in the right way. For example, we have seen that the author of the above argument had to believe that 'people don't already know about the effects on the environment of eating meat'. This is accurate and correct. If we had put, 'People don't already know about the effects of eating meat,' it would be incorrect. This statement is too general, not being focused on the specific demands of the argument. So would saying, 'People don't already know about how what we eat can affect the environment.' When we get to versions such as, 'People don't know enough about the environment,' we're getting way off focus (and should expect very few, if any, marks).

That's all the analysis done. You should now be able to find reasons, conclusions, counter-assertions/counter-claims, counter-arguments, evidence, examples, hypothetical reasoning, and assumptions.

# Evaluation of arguments

## Statistical evidence

The main area for evaluation in the Unit F501 paper is the central issue of considering whether or not reasons provide strong or only limited support for a conclusion.

We'll look at this shortly, but first we must deal with the evaluation of statistical evidence: you are expected to be competent in this. Statistical evidence is often used to support reasons or to draw conclusions. So how do we evaluate it?

We need to approach it in the same way as we would any other evidence. In other words, we need to ask questions about the significance of the evidence:

- What does/might the evidence mean?
- What meaning does the author give it?

These two questions cover many aspects of evaluation. This is because they lead us to ask all sorts of other questions:

- How has the author used the evidence?
- Are there explanations for the evidence that weaken/conflict with the way the author uses it?
- Is the evidence adequate for its purpose in the argument?
- What do we need to know about the evidence in order for it to be used in the way the author uses it?

Here's some evidence being used to support an argument:

> Young women don't seem to be influenced by campaigns to discourage them from sexual activity below the age of consent. In 1999, 25% of teenage girls had experienced underage sex. However, a 2006 poll carried out by Radio 1 found that of the 16- to 24-year-olds surveyed, 30% had had underage sex.

What can we say about this statistical evidence?

- It is certainly relevant to the content of the conclusion (first sentence).
- Though we know something about the 2006 poll (it was carried out by Radio 1), we don't know anything about the 1999 one.
- However, with regard to the Radio 1 poll, we don't know how it was carried out or how many people were asked.
- There is a crossover period between the two polls which might or might not be relevant. Thus, some of those surveyed in 2006 might also have been included in the 1999 survey.

## Questioning the evidence

Does it matter that we don't know anything about the 1999 poll? Yes, it does. In order to evaluate the significance of statistical evidence, we need to know how the information was obtained (including the way in which the questions were put and how many people were asked). For example, if the study was one in which young women filled in a questionnaire in a magazine, we could make at least two points. It could be that the magazine's readership wasn't very typical of young women in general. This could result in distortion of the 'real' picture. Also, the young women who responded to the questionnaire might not be typical of the wider readership.

Though we know something about the 2006 poll, we still need to ask questions about how the evidence was collected. Was it a phone-in poll? Was it done by text or e-mail? How many young women responded? Are the young women who listen to Radio 1 typical of all young women?

Both polls involve the issue of honesty. How do we know whether or not the young women in the surveys were telling the truth? It could be that most were, but we also have the possibilities of what we can call over- and under-claiming. In other words, young women might say they had had underage sex when they hadn't, or they might say they hadn't when they had. For obvious reasons, it's not an easy one to sort out!

(This problem of over- and under-claiming is relevant to many other surveys of behaviour and 'private' aspects of life. For example, surveys on alcohol usage could be distorted by young people over-claiming alcohol consumption and older people under-claiming it. The same could apply to surveys of spending, earning, illegal drug use, pornography use, and so on.)

## The conclusion and the evidence: alternative explanations

Another thing we can do is to look at the conclusion in relation to the evidence. The author sees the evidence as not only relevant to the conclusion but also sufficient for it. We've already looked at why the evidence might have problems, but is there also a problem with the conclusion?

> Young women don't seem to be influenced by campaigns to discourage them from sexual activity below the age of consent.

This conclusion does need statistical evidence. The best evidence might be a well-constructed survey on the specific issue the conclusion highlights: evidence showing whether young women were or were not influenced by these campaigns. Without this, the author merely infers from the rise in the percentage of young women having underage sex that the campaigns aren't working. But of course we could look for alternative explanations:

- Perhaps the campaigns are working with some young women, in that if there hadn't been the campaigns, the rate in 2006 would have been even higher than 30%.
- Perhaps the 1999 survey was inaccurate and the real figure was actually higher than 25% (perhaps even higher than 30%).
- Perhaps the 2006 survey was inaccurate and the real figure was actually lower than 30% (perhaps the same as, or even lower than, the 1999 survey).

(You may have noticed that we're back into assumptions here, with the author having to assume that none of the above is true. Try the negative test on them to see.)

## Samples

We've noted that we may need to take into account how many people were surveyed when we're judging statistical evidence. But it isn't necessarily a case of the bigger the better. We can have unreliable evidence from 2,000 people and reliable evidence from 1,000. We need to consider how the evidence was collected, rather than just the numbers involved.

Furthermore, we need to consider what proportion of the whole group was surveyed. If the whole group is itself not very big, then a survey of only a small number of people might well be adequate.

With very large groups there are more problems. For example, the editor of the girls' magazine *Bliss* said that a survey it did on teenage sexual behaviour involved '2,000 girls spread across the UK, which we thought was a pretty representative sample'. It could be that the 2,000 were indeed representative, but we would need to know (rather than 'think'). In other words, we'd need to look at whether the 2,000 as far as possible mirrored the population of girls generally in terms of education, occupation, regions, income levels, racial groups, religious groups, and so on.

This is something that a good survey organisation is very likely to get right. And by getting it right, they don't necessarily need to survey 2,000 people. So although you may be told that size matters, quality is more important: the quality of the sample surveyed in terms of how representative it is known to be.

## Over-generalisation

There does come a point, of course, where size has to matter. When you get down to very small numbers, there are likely to be problems if they are used to represent a much bigger number. This is the problem of **over-generalisation** (sometimes called 'hasty generalisation', which is misleading because 'hasty' suggests 'speedy' and this is not necessarily the case).

You might remember the publicity about 13-year-old Alfie Patten, who was allegedly the father of a baby born to 15-year-old Chantelle Stedman (and later reported not to be the father). The media seized on the case as evidence of what is referred to as 'broken Britain'. Here are two examples of how it was used in this way.

The first is from the *Daily Telegraph* of 13 February 2009:

> Anyone doubting that Britain is broken needs only to open yesterday's papers to see Alfie's dad, Dennis — father of nine, or possibly 10 children by various mothers — wearing a bizarre devil mask and brandishing a placard bearing the legend 'No Comment Ring Max', a reference to PR guru Max Clifford.

The second is from London's *Evening Standard* of 12 February 2009:

> Former Tory leader Iain Duncan Smith, who runs the Centre for Social Justice think tank, said: 'It's utterly tragic. It exemplifies the point we have been making about broken Britain...the complete collapse in some parts of society.'

You will see that in both reports, the evidence of this case is seen as more than an isolated example of pre-teenage and teenage fumbling. Alfie's dad Dennis is seen as sufficient evidence for 'broken Britain' by the *Daily Telegraph*. Iain Duncan Smith sees the case as sufficient reason to refer not only to 'broken Britain' but also to 'the complete collapse' of aspects of British society.

However, the case actually tells us very little about anything. Apart from the fact that its truth has subsequently been challenged, we can draw virtually no useful generalisations from it. It is not typical (if it were, then it wouldn't have been on all the front pages). So when the *Daily Star* announces 'Dad at 13. Welcome to broken Britain', we can sigh and move on.

# Do the reasons support the conclusion?

In addition to evaluating the use of statistical evidence, you are expected to be able to judge whether the conclusion of an argument is usefully supported by the reason(s). How can we do this?

You need to remember that in the arguments you'll be dealing with, there is *always* the question of whether the conclusion might require some other supporting reasoning. At most, we can say that the conclusion very probably follows from the reason(s) (rather than it *must* follow).

## Criteria

So what criteria should we use when we're asked to judge whether reasons adequately support conclusions?

It might be useful to work backwards with this. In other words, we'll start with a conclusion and consider what reasons (including evidence) could support it. Here's the conclusion:

> We should support strategies designed to reduce our use of plastic shopping bags.

Now we'll look at some potential reasons for this conclusion. Here's the first:

> It used to be said that there weren't any alternatives to plastic bags, but now there are plenty.

This both refers to a possible counter-position and responds to it. In that sense, it might be seen as providing some strength to the conclusion. The weakness is that it doesn't explain why plastic bags are a problem. In other words, just because there are alternatives to plastic bags, it doesn't mean we should use them. You can see that at least two assumptions are needed here to connect this as a reason with the conclusion.

- The alternatives to plastic bags do not have problems greater than those associated with plastic bags.
- Plastic bags create problems.

You can see that this second assumption will always be required if no reason detailing these problems is given.

We'll now look at the second possible reason:

> Ten billion plastic bags are handed out every year to UK shoppers (which is equivalent to 290 per person).

This has the same problem as the first statement. Alarming (and bizarre) though these statistics are, they're relevant only if, as before, plastic bags create problems. We could go with the simplest of the possible problems, that of waste (which must be a likely consequence of 10 billion bags).

Here's a third possible reason:

> Plastic bags are used in the UK for an average of 12 minutes (but take 500 years to degrade).

This has some strength as a reason in two ways. It picks up on the implied problem of waste in the second reason by giving us possibly relevant detail (only 12 minutes' average use). It also gives us information that can be used directly to support the conclusion. This is that plastic bags 'take 500 years to degrade', which is a reason not to use them. (The weakness, of course, is that we don't know about the time needed for the alternatives to degrade. This brings in a further assumption, that the alternatives do not take as long, or take longer.)

## Combining reasons

Now we can see how claims can give strength to each other. If we put the second and third claim together, we can see how they can usefully act to support the conclusion:

> Ten billion plastic bags are handed out every year to UK shoppers (which is equivalent to 290 per person). Plastic bags are used in the UK for an average of 12 minutes (but take 500 years to degrade). We should support strategies designed to reduce our use of plastic shopping bags.

Putting the two claims together as two reasons shows us that the power of the two together is greater than twice the power of the two acting separately.

Perhaps we could even add the first claim we considered, now that we've provided the necessary reasoning to give it significance:

> Ten billion plastic bags are handed out every year to UK shoppers (which is equivalent to 290 per person). Plastic bags are used in the UK for an average of 12 minutes (but take 500 years to degrade). It used to be said that there weren't any alternatives to plastic bags, but now there are plenty. We should support strategies designed to reduce our use of plastic shopping bags.

What about a third claim?

> In Ireland, a tax of 15 cents (about 13p) was put on all supermarket plastic bags, which led to a decrease of 90% in their use.

On its own, does this add anything? It is certainly relevant to the issue of strategies designed to reduce the use of plastic bags, in that it provides evidence (an example that can be used as evidence) of a strategy that had some success. But, of course, it doesn't give us a reason why we should support such strategies. Just because something can be done, it doesn't mean we should do it.

## Relevance of reasons

Though the example of Ireland could play a part in dealing with a possible counter-argument that strategies don't work, putting this claim on its own as a reason for the conclusion is a problem:

> In Ireland, a tax of 15 cents (about 13p) was put on all supermarket plastic bags, which led to a decrease of 90% in their use. We should support strategies designed to reduce our use of plastic shopping bags.

As you can see, one of the most effective ways to judge the power of reasons is to look for **relevance**. We need to focus on what the conclusion is essentially about. In this case, it's obviously about plastic bags, but essentially it's about the need to *reduce* our use of them. That's the core point. So claims have to be relevant to that core point if they are to serve as good, strong reasons.

So we could use the evidence/example of Ireland to take the argument a stage further:

> Ten billion plastic bags are handed out every year to UK shoppers (which is equivalent to 290 per person). Plastic bags are used in the UK for an average of 12 minutes (but take 500 years to degrade). We should support strategies designed to reduce our use of plastic shopping bags. In Ireland, a tax of 15 cents (about 13p) was put on all supermarket plastic bags, which led to a decrease of 90% in their use. Therefore the government should tax plastic bags in order to help reduce their use.

This is impressive. The evidence of Ireland now works well as a reason for a new conclusion. It's nicely focused on the two essential points of 'tax' and 'reduce'.

So when you're asked to evaluate the reasons used in an argument, you're looking for relevance in terms of the essential point of the conclusion.

## Consistency of reasons

Another thing you're looking for is **consistency**.

The following information might be a problem for the above argument:

> Paper bags are more of a problem for global warming than are plastic bags. They take up more space than plastic bags and therefore use up more energy in being transported.

It's a problem if the author leaves paper bags as something preferable to plastic bags. Or is it? Well, this depends on why the author is arguing that we should reduce our use of plastic bags. The argument that we constructed was centred on the need to reduce this use because of the problem of disposing of the bags. In this way, it wasn't necessarily anything to do with energy use and global warming. The author of our argument might brush this issue aside:

> Ten billion plastic bags are handed out every year to UK shoppers (which is equivalent to 290 per person). Plastic bags are used in the UK for an average of 12 minutes (but take 500 years to degrade). Though it has been shown that paper bags are more of a problem for global warming than are plastic bags because they take up more space than plastic bags and therefore use up more energy in being transported, the important issue here isn't global warming, but waste disposal. We should support strategies designed to reduce our use of plastic shopping bags.

So, if we're going to use consistency as a criterion for judging reasoning, then we have to make sure we're reading the argument in the right way.

What about the next statement?

> Producing plastic bags requires large amounts of oil (430,000 gallons to make 100 million bags), and oil is a non-renewable resource.

This would fit well with the demand for consistency. It is in the same direction as the conclusion ('reduce our use of plastic bags') and in fact lends some strong support to it (especially with the information on high use of a non-renewable resource).

## Conflation

Consistency is also a factor in how an author uses words. This might seem somewhat obscure, but it can arise in material that you're asked to look at. In other words, the question paper might include an example in which an author is guilty of inconsistency in the use of language.

Look at the next example:

> There's a lot of talk about people using their leisure time in ways that will be more beneficial to them. Unfortunately, there are all sorts of reasons why this is difficult to achieve. Going to watch live sports events is too expensive for many people, with ticket prices for Premier League football matches and those for international cricket events being too high for many to afford on a regular basis. There's also the fact that major sporting events (like Premier League matches and Test cricket) are shown on satellite channels. Thus encouraging people to get out and about more will not work unless these problems are addressed.

In this argument, the author starts by talking about getting people to use their 'leisure' time in more beneficial ways. However, the conclusion is concerned with the need to 'encourage people to get out and about more'. The author has thus taken 'leisure' and 'getting out and about' to mean the same thing. But they do not, because, for example, people might happily use their leisure time watching football on television. This problem of taking one term or word to be equivalent to another (when they are not equivalent) is called **conflation**. Watch out for it.

## Additional reasons

As well as being asked to evaluate the reasons in an argument, you might be asked to come up with an additional reason for an argument. In doing this, you need to use the same criteria of relevance and consistency that we have looked at in evaluating reasoning. This is because a useful additional reason is one that is both relevant to and consistent with the rest of the argument.

Here's an example of a claim that, because it's both relevant and consistent, could be used as an additional reason:

> Plastic bags are a danger to wildlife because animals can get trapped in them or swallow bits of them.

So you've now got all the skills needed to complete Section A of the Unit F501 paper. That's 35 of the marks under your belt.

# Credibility of evidence
## Credibility criteria

Much of what we do in critical thinking is about looking at claims and evaluating how they are, or might be, used. So when we're asked to look at claims in terms of their credibility, is this different from what we're doing when we're looking for alternative explanations and so on?

Importantly, no, it's not. We're still looking at the significance of claims and judging whether an author can use them as they do. All we're doing differently is to use additional ways of evaluating claims. This is done by using what you will have learned as **credibility criteria**.

Credibility is, of course, just another word for 'believability'. What we're asking is: How believable is that claim? Is it more or less believable than another one? Why?

So what do we mean by a **credibility criterion** ('criterion' being the singular of criteria)? A criterion is a standard by which something can be judged or evaluated. A credibility criterion is thus a standard by which the believability of claims can be judged.

You can see that these criteria are different from the other ways in which we have so far been evaluating claims. We haven't yet worried about whether we should believe a claim. We've just got on with looking at whether, if true, it's got the significance the author intends.

But now we're into possible distortions, omissions, even lies. Let's just remind ourselves of the credibility criteria we're meant to use.

## Plausibility

The exam paper wants you to look at **plausibility**. What is meant by this? Recent question papers tried to help you to understand this by explaining it as 'likelihood'. Unfortunately, they're not always the same thing. When you're looking at whether one version of events is more or less plausible than another, you could consider likelihood and ask, 'How likely is it that X or Y happened?' But if you're being asked to compare the plausibility of two cases, one for and the other against, then the question clearly cannot be approached in terms of how likely one case is compared to the other.

Fortunately, plausibility has an entirely straightforward meaning: *reasonableness*. So you wouldn't talk about 'plausibility and reasonableness of claims' as if they're two separate things. Always remember that if you're asked to judge whether a claim is plausible, you're being asked to judge whether it's reasonable. Is it such that it's not absurd, not beyond what we might believe to have happened? If a *case* is being presented, then *plausibility* doesn't mean *likelihood*: it means *reasonableness*.

Look at the following example:

> In November 2008, an 8-year-old boy in Phoenix, Arizona confessed to murdering his father and another man. Although at first he denied killing them, after an hour of police questioning he admitted the crime. He claimed that he found them already wounded, so shot his father to put him out of his suffering.

How plausible is this? How reasonable is it to believe either that an 8-year-old boy shot his father and the lodger, or that he shot them after having found them already wounded by a previous shooting? Given that we're looking at the plausibility of an *event*, in this account we could usefully ask about the likelihood of the event.

But the case was newsworthy for another reason, beyond the plausibility of the claimed description of events. This was because the police wanted the boy prosecuted as an adult, and charged him with premeditated murder. Many people were opposed to this:

> Various legal experts have argued that the boy should not and indeed cannot be tried as an adult. His apparent 'confession' was obtained in circumstances which did not follow the correct procedure (there was no lawyer present during the questioning). In addition, as the director of a law psychiatry programme at a US university has pointed out, 'I have never heard of an eight-year-old being tried as an adult. It would be more than extraordinary. It would be totally unique.'

In this passage, we read that there are reasons why the boy should not be tried as an adult. If we ask, 'Is this plausible?' we're not asking, 'Is this likely?' because the latter question makes no sense. Is what likely? That the boy will or won't be tried as an adult? But that isn't the point.

So there you have it. When you are looking at *events*, things that happened, and you're being asked for plausibility, you can see reasonableness in terms of *likelihood*. When you're dealing with two different *cases* for something, then plausibility cannot mean 'likelihood', it means simply *reasonableness*.

Having dealt with the meaning of plausibility, we'll now clarify the meaning of the other credibility criteria.

## Bias

**Bias** is used in two ways, although the two are connected. The first is when claims are made in a selective way. This can sometimes be called 'cherry-picking' in the sense that a person or an organisation chooses only the most favourable parts of a case in order to argue for their position.

It can also be used to mean that a person or an organisation is likely to take a particular position because they favour it. Thus we would expect that the Huntingdon Life Sciences (HLS) organisation, which carries out research using experiments on animals, would always favour the argument that animal experiments are necessary for medical science. It is straightforwardly biased in that direction (just as SHAC — Stop Huntingdon Animal Cruelty — is straightforwardly biased against it).

You can see, though, that the two meanings of the term normally can't be kept apart. HLS will make selective claims, will cherry-pick the evidence, *because* it comes to the debate from a particular position.

The two meanings could be kept separate when the bias is not deliberate. This could arise in situations where claims are made which are based on inadequate evidence. For example, an account of events written by someone unable to see or hear all the evidence would be biased in this way.

However, this non-deliberate bias is unlikely to be the thing that you're asked to look for in the exam paper. So we're looking for selective accounts which are *a result of* the author being predisposed to a particular position.

## Vested interest

How might bias be different from another criterion that's used — **vested interest**? Vested interest is clearly a type of bias, but what type? And what type of bias isn't vested interest? It's quite difficult to unravel these two. We have seen that HLS will be biased in the way it deals with information on animal experimentation. But the bias will come not only from the work that it specialises in, but also from the fact that it earns its money in this way. It has a financial interest in having its position presented and accepted.

So is there a useful distinction that we can apply? The difference is that vested interest is supposed to be present when the possibility of gain can lead to biased claims. This gain could be financial (as in the case of HLS). It could benefit someone's career or their position. It could enable someone to achieve something at another's expense. Bias, on the other hand, includes situations where there is no obvious vested interest.

Importantly, of course, vested interest might bias a person or an organisation towards telling the truth. In this situation, the term retains its meaning of benefit gained from acting in a particular way. We can think of plenty of examples in which vested interest will lead *X* to tell the truth.

- Somebody might have a vested interest in telling the truth because if they were found to be lying, the consequences would be really bad for them.
- Somebody might have a strong belief in the need always to tell the truth, and so would feel very upset if they lied.
- An organisation might have a vested interest in telling the truth because the truth is beneficial to it (and/or damaging to a rival organisation).
- A person or an organisation might have a vested interest in telling the truth because they have a good reputation for being truthful which they don't want to damage.

It is simple enough to reverse any of the above to list situations in which a person or an organisation might have a vested interest in not telling the truth.

## Motive and expertise

In short, then, we can see both bias and vested interest as part of **motive**. Someone has a motive to act in a certain way (tell the truth, lie, report only part of the evidence) for some reason (benefit to them, of whatever type — this is how they're expected to act, and so on).

When we gave the example of HLS, we saw it as an example of bias. HLS is biased towards animal experimentation. It would make no sense if it wasn't. But the bias has to be seen in connection with other credibility criteria. One of these is **expertise**. By this we mean training, experience and knowledge. This expertise is often seen as a very strong criterion, such that those who have it are likely to be more credible than those without it. Thus HLS has expertise in the area of medical experiments on animals.

## Using credibility criteria

You can begin to see that using credibility criteria is a bit like playing Top Trumps. A criterion such as expertise will often (perhaps even normally) trump one such as vested interest. But there are many factors to consider.

### Expertise

Here's an example:

> Professor Johannes Doehmer from the Technical University of Munich told a conference in November 2008 that using animals in medical experiments to predict what would happen in humans was simply not scientifically valid. As he put it, there is 'no more place for animal studies'.

We have a clear example of expertise here. One does not get to be a professor at this university in Munich without qualifications and experience. (His qualifications are in genetics and biochemistry.) Professor Doehmer is clearly an expert. But is that the end of the matter?

We also know that, as well as being a professor at the Technical University of Munich, he serves as scientific advisor to the company BioProof. This specialises in research into drugs. Do we need to know whether BioProof specialises in medical research which doesn't involve animals? We do, if we think that what Professor Doehmer says about animals in medical research is biased because of vested interest. We need to stress, however, that just because he is scientific advisor to this company doesn't mean that what he says is either biased or is an example of vested interest. It could well be that his expertise is always going to be the trump card.

What about those experts who take a different position? People who had won Nobel Prizes in physiology and medicine were the subject of a survey. All 71 living prize winners were sent questionnaires, and 39 replied. From these 39 the following results were obtained:
- Ninety-seven per cent 'strongly agreed' that 'animal experiments have been vital to the discovery and development of many advances in physiology and medicine'. (The other 3% 'agreed'.)
- Ninety-two per cent 'strongly agreed' that 'animal experiments are still crucial to the investigation and development of many medical treatments'. (The other 8% 'agreed'.)

Thinking back for a minute to what we considered when we were looking at statistical evidence, you could look at these figures and say something about them in relation to the sample. Is the fact that only 39 out of 71 (55%) replied significant? Might it be that the other 32 thought differently (or at least that a large number of them did)?

But is the expertise of these people the main thing? The people who did the study obviously thought so. (We'll come to who they are shortly.) To get a Nobel Prize, you have to be recognised as a very important expert in your field, as judged by the thousands of qualified people who are asked to make nominations. So in the credibility game of Top Trumps, you would think that a Nobel Prize winner (technically called a Nobel Laureate) would trump any other expert in their field. This is where Top Trumps starts getting complicated. Perhaps the Nobel Laureates were people who worked many years ago (they do tend to be rather old), when there weren't useful alternatives to using animals in medical research (such as mathematical models, computer models, genetic analysis and using human cells). Perhaps there are other explanations.

And, as promised, you might be interested to know who had the research on Nobel Laureates carried out. This was Patients' Voice for Medical Advance (also known as Patients' Voice), an organisation that supports 'humane' medical research using animals. So are we now into bias, including vested interest?

We have been looking at examples in which the expertise is very relevant to the subject being considered. This is an important point. Newspaper columnists regularly comment on a wide range of topics. For example, Libby Purves in *The Times* writes on subjects as diverse as the Church of England, vegetarianism, Josef Fritzl (the Austrian who kept his daughter in a cellar for many years), politics, crime, education and poetry. She and her fellow journalists are not necessarily experts in all these matters, so we should not look to them for expert pronouncements on all subjects.

There is also the point that while a person or organisation might well have considerable expertise, it isn't always relevant to the issue they're commenting on. Thus a qualified medical doctor will have expertise in health matters but not necessarily in economics. A religious organisation might have expertise in matters of faith, but not necessarily in the theory of evolution. So when we're using expertise as a criterion to show the strength of evidence, we need to make sure that it's relevant to the evidence.

### Ability to perceive

Another important credibility criterion is the **ability to perceive**. You'll often see this also described as the 'ability to see', but this is less helpful. Quite simply, the ability to perceive includes the ability to see, hear and feel, so why should we narrow it to only 'seeing'? It might even be better to define this criterion as the 'ability to experience', but the exam board doesn't use that term, so neither should you.

How are we to use this criterion? The most obvious way is to use it when referring to someone who saw, heard, etc., something (especially an event) because they were sufficiently close to it. You will often notice that a television reporter covering an event such as an accident will interview someone who claims to have seen it happen. Their evidence is seen as especially important, and in some ways, of course, it is.

However, there are problems with such evidence, because even those who were sufficiently close to the event may have experienced only part of it, and may have been distracted by something while it was happening. They may even have been distressed or confused. To make things potentially even more difficult, they may remember what they experienced in a selective way. You will need to note that these problems could weaken the significance of the criterion of ability to perceive.

The exam board rightly distinguishes between 'primary' and 'secondary' evidence. The first is evidence given by those with the ability to perceive; secondary evidence is the reporting of primary evidence. You can see that while distortions can arise even with primary evidence, they can be increased with secondary evidence. For example, someone might be selective in reporting the content of primary evidence because they have a vested interest.

We can usefully distinguish between primary and secondary evidence, but there is also a problem with how the examiners sometimes use it. They might use the criterion of ability to perceive in a way that does not distinguish between the two. Thus they sometimes present a person reading a report on something as an example of the ability to perceive. Though we can see that someone reading a report has the ability to perceive the report, there are problems with using the criterion in this way. For example, someone might read a report but not (fully) understand it. In addition, someone might read a selectively written (biased) report and read it in a biased way (noting only those parts that they agreed with). So should the criterion be used in this way? Straightforwardly, no. Should you use it in this way? Straightforwardly, yes. This is what is required for the exam.

## Neutrality

We have seen that expertise and ability to perceive are both potentially strong criteria in the Top Trumps game. Here's another: **neutrality**. This is effectively the opposite of bias. A person or organisation that isn't biased will be seen as neutral. An account of something that isn't selective will be seen as neutral.

For centuries justice has been symbolised by the figure of a female figure holding a sword and a pair of scales. The sword represents the power of the law to punish; the scales symbolise the way in which courts should operate, by judging according to the weight of evidence. But the figure has another feature: she is blindfolded. This emphasises the fact that justice should be impartial. Judgements should be made only on the basis of the evidence.

In the same way, if we identify a source (whether this is one or more people or an organisation) as neutral, then we are claiming that they have (or have had) no links with either side of a dispute which could affect their position.

A US court case in 2005 provides an interesting example of how expertise can possibly be affected by a lack of neutrality:

> Timothy Wilkins was on trial, accused of acting as a drug mule (someone who smuggles drugs for others). The psychologist appointed by the defence reported to the court that Mr Wilkins had an IQ of 58 and so, because he did not understand the court proceedings, should not stand trial. However, the psychologist appointed by the prosecution reported to the court that Mr Wilkins had an IQ of 88 and so, because he understood the proceedings, should stand trial. The judge ruled out both reports because, as he put it, they 'cancelled each other out'. Mr Wilkins' lawyer agreed. 'One's biased for the defence. The other's biased for the state. I think it's who's signing their paycheck.'

Even if we can identify a source as neutral, it might well be that their evidence is used in a biased way. Thus we might be able to find that evidence collected and analysed by a neutral source is selectively used by another source in support of their own position.

## Credibility criteria in combination

At this stage we can note that credibility criteria gain strength or add to weakness by acting together.

What combination could give us very strong reasons to believe the evidence?

**Relevant expertise + ability to perceive + neutrality = more credible source**

What combination could give us very strong reasons to doubt the evidence?

**Lack of relevant expertise + lack of ability to perceive + bias (including vested interest) = less credible source**

Let's see if we can add to these equations with further criteria.

### Reputation

Another criterion that's used is that of **reputation**. This is an unusual one in that it's based on other people's judgement of the source. When we're assessing expertise, we look for relevant qualifications and/or experience: HLS, for example, clearly has expertise in using animals in medical experiments. In the case of ability to perceive, a source either had it or it hadn't. (They either had sufficient access to $X$, or they didn't.) When we're considering vested interest, it might be less clear-cut, but we can identify factors such as the benefit that a source might derive from giving evidence one way or the other (as with the psychologists in the Timothy Wilkins case).

However, when we're looking at reputation it's a matter of judgement rather than of identification. And there's another difference between reputation and the other criteria: the reputation criterion is used on the basis of past performance. When this criterion is used, we're saying that what happened in the past affects our judgement of the present credibility of a source. We will say things like, 'The BBC has a good reputation for being fair in its reporting of the middle east, as shown by its refusal to broadcast an appeal for a Palestinian fund.' In this example, we are using the *previous* behaviour of the BBC as evidence for a *present* judgement of its reputation for being unbiased.

It could be that certain *groups* are seen as having a reputation, either good or bad. This is again normally based on past performance. However, it's by no means certain which groups these are. Presumably medical doctors might be seen as having a positive reputation (despite examples such as the convicted murderer Harold Shipman). What about the police? Presumably a mixture of good and bad reputation. What about nurses? Generally a good reputation, presumably. Social workers? (Baby P etc? Perhaps not so good.) MPs? (A bit of a mixture there.)

You can see that using the reputation card can be a problem in that you're likely to have to justify why you think a source has a good or a bad reputation. You can argue this in terms of how the source is seen (by the public, fellow experts, and so on) and/or how their past performance has contributed to the reputation, whether it's good or bad. So, if we're adding this criterion to the equations we looked at earlier, we need to be clear about why our source has a good or a bad reputation.

**Relevant expertise + ability to perceive + neutrality + positive reputation = more credible source**

**Lack of relevant expertise + lack of ability to perceive + bias (including vested interest) + negative reputation = less credible source**

## Corroboration

But we're not finished yet. There's one more aspect of credibility that we need to consider. It might be seen as giving us two credibility criteria, even though it's just the positive and negative sides of the same one. You will probably have seen these as **corroboration** and **inconsistency** (or **conflict**).

Corroboration is based on the idea that the significance of evidence is strengthened if more than one source reports it. This is unremarkable. We would be more impressed by a scientific or historical claim if more than one study reported it. For example, the claim that there is less global warming than is generally believed would be strengthened if we had a lot of evidence (polar bears not declining in numbers, the Antarctic getting colder, etc.). In court, the way the evidence stacks up one way or the other makes a case stronger or weaker. Thus Steve Wright, the 'Suffolk Strangler', was convicted on the basis of an accumulation of evidence (DNA evidence, fibres of clothing, photographic evidence, and so on) which all pointed in the direction of his guilt.

If we return to the issue of plausibility, we could say that having more than one source reporting the same or a similar thing makes a case, version or position more plausible.

Charles Darwin produced a mass of evidence which led him to develop the theory of natural selection. For him, the separate pieces of evidence (whether regarding birds, plants, animals or insects) all pointed in the same direction. The corroboration that each piece of evidence gave served to strengthen (make more plausible) the explanation he was putting forward.

## Inconsistency

A lack of corroboration could therefore be seen as a weakness (although it doesn't have to mean that the evidence is weak). But this lack would be much more significant if there were conflicting evidence pointing us in a different direction. The difference between the psychologists' results in the Timothy Wilkins case is a good example.

The criterion of inconsistency has another use beyond conflicting evidence. This is when there is inconsistency *within* the evidence given by a source. The following gives an example:

> Aircraft noise in the area has increased substantially over the past ten years, such that it has become a significant problem for the residents living under the flight path. People trying to sell their homes have had great problems in attracting buyers. Furthermore, the number of people moving away from the area because of the noise has trebled over the past five years, with all sorts of implications for the communities, such as the survival of local schools and shops.

The author claims that people are finding it difficult to sell their houses, but also that there has been a trebling in the number of people moving away. Though these two claims might not necessarily be inconsistent (for example, perhaps the people moving away were renting their homes), they could be seen (without further information) as being inconsistent, and thus the report is weakened.

Let's now add corroboration and inconsistency/conflict to our earlier equations:

**Relevant expertise + ability to perceive + neutrality + positive reputation = more credible source**

**Credible source + corroboration from other credible source(s) = more credible report**

**Lack of relevant expertise + lack of ability to perceive + bias (including vested interest) + negative reputation = less credible source**

**Less credible source + inconsistency with other source(s) = less credible report**

There are, of course, variations in these equations. A report that is corroborated by a source that has poor credibility gains little (and might lose much) in terms of its own credibility. Similarly, a credible report that is inconsistent with a source that has poor credibility might not thereby be weakened (and might even be strengthened).

## Applying credibility criteria

So what do you have to do with these credibility criteria?
- You need to be able to use these criteria in such a way that you understand what they mean.
- You need to be able to apply them to sources and reports in such a way that you can use them to assess the credibility of these sources and reports.
- You need to be able to suggest further information needed in order to support any assessment of credibility you have already made.
- You need to be able to consider the credibility of both sides of a dispute and to produce a 'reasoned case' (argument) to show which of the two is the more plausible (reasonable).

That's it, then. You now have all the skills needed to complete Section B of the Unit F501 paper. That's the other 40 marks under your belt.

But before we have a look at how you should apply your skills to the questions, we'll just remind ourselves of the list of terms you're expected to know in answering them:

- argument
- reason
- conclusion
- assumption
- counter-argument
- counter-assertion/ counter-claim

- evidence and example
- hypothetical reasoning/reason/ argument
- consistency and inconsistency

- bias
- vested interest
- motive
- reputation
- expertise
- ability to perceive
- neutrality

# Questions
# &
# Answers

In the examination, you'll be given a resource booklet which will contain numbered 'documents' and any background information you are likely to need in order to understand the content of these documents. You'll also be given the question paper. This will be divided into Section A and Section B.

You will have 1 hour 30 minutes in all to do the paper. You are advised on the front of the question paper to divide this time into three parts: about 10 minutes reading the resource booklet, about 30 minutes doing the questions in Section A, about 45 minutes doing the questions in Section B. (These don't add up to exactly 90 minutes, but they give guidance on the way you should allocate your time.)

This needs some explaining. As we have seen, Section A carries 35 of the marks, with Section B giving the other 40. So why should you spend 30 minutes getting 35 marks but 45 minutes getting 40 marks?

The answer is simple: it must be easier to get the marks in Section A than those in Section B. And it probably is, for two reasons.

First, you can get a lot of marks in Section A simply for stating what's already there, by reading the material. For example, you can get 3 marks for no more than accurately stating the conclusion of an argument. You can also get 3 marks for stating a reason used in an argument (thus 6 marks for stating two). Similarly, you can get 3 marks for stating the conclusion of a counter-argument, with another 3 for giving its reason.

Second, in Section B you are doing much more evaluation and you're having to do this by thinking of the criteria that are appropriate. Thus more judgement is involved, and it is often less clear exactly what you should be writing.

What follows is a detailed guide to the sort of questions that you might expect in the exam. Answers to these questions are given, some perfect (to show how to get full marks) and some less so, with explanations of why the marks are likely to be reduced. You'll find first of all a set of documents, and then some questions based on these documents. As you might expect in the exam paper, before the documents are presented you will find some background information which should answer any questions you might have about the content of the documents.

# Resources booklet

## Background information

People for the Ethical Treatment of Animals (PETA) has more than 2 million members and supporters, and is thus the largest animal rights organisation in the world. According to PETA, it focuses on 'the four areas in which the largest numbers of animals suffer the most intensely for the longest periods of time: on factory farms, in laboratories, in the clothing trade, and in the entertainment industry'. (It includes zoos in the fourth category.)

The British and Irish Association of Zoos and Aquariums (BIAZA) is the organisation that represents what it claims are the 'best' zoos in Britain and Ireland. It argues that it sees the promotion of good welfare for zoo animals as a priority.

The *International Zoo Yearbook* is an international forum for the exchange of information on the role of zoos in the conservation of species and habitats. It is published by the Zoological Society of London as a service to zoos around the world.

Zoologists are biologists who study animals.

Kudus are a type of antelope.

The *Independent* is a daily UK newspaper.

### Document 1

It is often claimed by zoos that without them, many species would disappear. Such species include tigers and rhinos. This is because the conservation and captive breeding programmes in zoos help to preserve endangered species. However, zoos should not be seen as being concerned with the interests of animals. The main purpose of zoos is to make money for their owners. Captive breeding programmes help them to make money because people like to come and see recently born animals such as elephants and rhinos. Furthermore, animals in zoos often lead highly stressful lives. They are restricted in small enclosures and deprived of stimulation. Even the apparently large enclosures sometimes provided for elephants cannot begin to provide the range of 30 miles per day that these animals normally cover.

### Document 2

BIAZA stresses that in the wild, many animals suffer from attacks by predators, starvation, disease, parasites, cold and heat. Well-designed zoo enclosures can minimise, even eliminate, all these factors. In addition, BIAZA makes the point that the daily lives of zoo animals can be enriched by the provision of enhanced environments if zoos employ highly skilled and imaginative staff. BIAZA strongly claims that zoos 'meet the needs of the animals in their care by understanding what constitutes good welfare, and by providing appropriate housing and husbandry'. Thus zoos, it argues, improve the welfare of animals compared to their lives in the wild.

BIAZA coordinates research activities in zoos and considers studies in animal welfare a priority. Results from research are published in publications such as the *International Zoo Yearbook*.

Many of the members of BIAZA are world-famous zoos, such as London Zoo and Whipsnade, and these specialise in conservation activities in areas where endangered species live. Some species, such as the African black rhino, would not survive without some degree of management, including taking some animals into captivity.

## Document 3

PETA has highlighted research carried out by scientists at Oxford University which showed that animals suffer in zoos. They live in 'enclosures' which are much smaller than they would have in the wild. Polar bears, lions, tigers, elephants, cheetahs and other animals that would roam for many miles in the wild become stressed and miserable in their restricted enclosures.

PETA stresses that although zoos claim to contribute to conservation, they actually take money away from useful conservation projects in the wild. Instead of people paying money to see animals in cages and enclosures, they should be encouraged to give money to help animals survive in their natural habitats.

It has discovered that the Dickerson Park Zoo in the USA sold or 'donated' a giraffe, a kudu, five kangaroos and two deer to Buddy Jordan, an 'animal dealer who sells animals to exotic-animal auctions and breeders, unaccredited zoos, and even hunting ranches'. It stresses that 'babies born at the zoo should not end up as trophies on a hunter's wall'.

## Document 4

The *Independent* reports that 'elephants kept in zoos die younger than in the wild'. The research was published in the highly respected journal *Science*. The zoologists who did the research studied more than 4,500 African and Asian female elephants kept in zoos or living in the wild. The research showed that those elephants born in captivity had the lowest life expectancy of all, shorter even than those elephants that were captured in the wild and taken to zoos. It also showed that zoos need to have elephants taken from the wild in order to keep their breeding programmes going. As a result, it can be seen that elephants should not be kept in zoos.

# Question 1

**(a) State the main conclusion of the argument presented in Document 1.**

**(b) State the two reasons that are given to support the main conclusion in Document 1.**

**(c) State the counter-argument presented in Document 1.**
- **Counter-conclusion**
- **Counter-reason**

This would be a familiar set of questions at the beginning of a paper. They are straight-forward analysis questions. You will be asked to 'use the exact words of the author in your answers' to these questions.

For each question, 3 marks are available, with 2 and 1 also available for varying degrees of inadequacy (together with 0 marks for complete inadequacy).

So what answers are being looked for?

**(a) State the main conclusion of the argument presented in Document 1.**

Zoos should not be seen as being concerned with the interests of animals.

> You may remember that when we looked at what we're doing when we're trying to find the main conclusion of an argument, we asked the 'What's going on?' question. This would have worked here as we focused on the author's point that zoos shouldn't be seen as good for animals.
>
> There was also the point that a word such as *however* or *but* often indicates that the author is starting their argument, having already given a counter-position. Again, you would have found this useful here.
>
> You will see that the answer we gave satisfies the requirement to give the exact words. This is what the author says — no more and no less. So we get the full 3 marks. (You might want to query whether the word *however* in the sentence should have been included. The word isn't technically part of the conclusion, so you shouldn't include it. But you'll be pleased to hear that you wouldn't be penalised if you did.)
>
> What might count as a 2-mark answer?

Zoos are not concerned with the interests of animals.

> In this version, part of the original has been omitted, so it is not entirely accurate. The same comment would apply to the next version:

Zoos should not be seen as being concerned with animals.

> And for 1 mark?

Zoos aren't interested in animals.

> This answer misunderstands the word 'interests' in the conclusion, although it still has the thrust of the anti-zoo conclusion.
>
> And for 0 marks? Anything which gives the wrong part of the argument.

**(b) State the two reasons that are given to support the main conclusion in Document 1.**

The main purpose of zoos is to make money for their owners.

Animals in zoos often lead highly stressful lives.

> In each case, we have given only what is needed. In the second, you will see that we have missed out the word 'furthermore', because all it is doing is *signalling* a further reason. As before, however, you would not be penalised if you included the word.
>
> What we have written would attract 3 marks per answer (thus 6 in total). As with the discussion of the conclusion, as the answers become less accurate the marks start to decline from 2 to 1 to 0.
>
> The obvious things that would distract you are evidence, examples and development. There's plenty of this. For example, if you had written any of the following, you would be providing material relevant to the reasons but not the reasons themselves. In each case you would have been given no marks.

Captive breeding programmes help them to make money because people like to come and see recently born animals such as elephants and rhinos.

They are restricted in small enclosures and deprived of stimulation.

Even the apparently large enclosures sometimes provided for elephants cannot begin to provide the range of 30 miles per day that these animals normally cover.

> However, if you had put:

The main purpose of zoos is to make money

> you would have been given 2 marks (for being accurate in the wording but having missed out part of the reason).
>
> If you had given the reason correctly, but had added something which wasn't part of the reason, then your mark would fall to 1, as in the next example:

Animals in zoos often lead highly stressful lives. They are restricted in small enclosures and deprived of stimulation.

> Thus it is seen as a lesser sin to be accurate but incomplete than to be accurate but not to know where to stop. Don't forget!

**(c) State the counter-argument presented in Document 1.**
- **Counter-conclusion**
- **Counter-reason**

> Interestingly, the examiner is allowed a gesture of generosity when it comes to counter-arguments. If you had used the counter-argument as *the* argument, in the sense of using its reasoning for the previous question, then they are allowed to credit this. The justification for this generosity is that you would have demonstrated the skill of analysing an argument. However, the right answers are as follows.

**Counter-conclusion**

Without zoos, many species would disappear.

> As you can see, we have had to rejig the first sentence a little to get to this. We've done this because the author was presenting the conclusion in a way that fitted with introducing the subject. The examiner would therefore have been happy with this:

(It is often claimed by zoos that) without them, many species would disappear.

> Three marks, then. However, as you would expect, they would not have been happy with your adding 'Such species include tigers and rhinos', so the mark falls from 3 to 1. This is because, of course, that isn't part of the conclusion; it is merely given as an example.

**Counter-reason**

(This is because) their conservation and captive breeding programmes help to preserve endangered species.

> The tolerance of the words in brackets remains for the 3 marks.

> In any of these analysis questions the examiner has the opportunity to give a candidate 1 mark out of the 3 for getting the *gist* of the right answer. Giving only the gist suggests that the candidate has decided to paraphrase the wording of the passage. You're specifically told not to do this, and there are two good reasons why you shouldn't. (I know that I paraphrased the conclusion of the counter-argument above, but that was to present it more *accurately* by stating it as it would have been stated if it wasn't just being reported.)

> The first reason is that you're being asked to *state* the conclusion, reason, etc. You're being asked to state what the author has said, not to give a different version of it. Paraphrasing means that you're going to state it differently, with the risk that you give an inaccurate version.

> The second is that paraphrasing takes more time than merely stating! You're having to give thought to how to put it differently, whereas you should be simply writing it down and moving on. Save your paraphrasing skills for situations where you need them and will be rewarded for using them.

> An alternative question (c) could ask you to identify an example or a piece of evidence in the material:

**(c) State one example that is used to support the argument in Document 1.**

(Recently-born) Elephants and rhinos.

> This example is certainly given to support the claim (itself a piece of evidence) about captive breeding programmes.

> The example of elephants given in the final sentence of Document 1 would be an alternative answer.

# Question 2

**Paragraph 1 of Document 2 claims that 'the daily lives of zoo animals can be enriched by the provision of enhanced environments if zoos employ highly skilled and imaginative staff.'**

**(a) Name the argument element used.**

Hypothetical reason (or hypothetical reasoning).

> For writing two words we get 2 marks! This is probably the quickest way to get 2 marks anywhere on the paper.
>
> How might this be reduced to just 1 mark? By being incomplete or inaccurate. For example, if you just put 'reason', although you are in one important sense right (that's what it is in the sequence of the argument), you haven't described it sufficiently fully. Similarly, if you just put 'hypothetical', then your answer is incomplete. It would be inaccurate to say that it's a 'hypothetical argument', because this sentence is not the full argument.
>
> To get 0 marks, you would have to describe it wrongly (e.g. as 'evidence' or 'conclusion').

**(b) Explain your answer to 2(a).**

> You will remember that we looked at this task when we were discussing hypothetical reasoning earlier. Part of us wants to say no more than 'it has the *if...then* form of hypothetical reasoning', but unfortunately the examiner is not going to give their 2 marks away anything like as easily as before. (They should give you 1 for that, however.) For this question, you've got to give them chapter and verse.

It is a reason that includes a consequence ('the daily lives of zoo animals can be enriched by the provision of enhanced environments') which depends on the fulfilment of a condition (zoos employing 'highly skilled and imaginative staff').

> As well as giving only 1 mark for only explaining that it is in hypothetical form, the examiner could give 1 for only explaining why it is a reason that supports the conclusion.
>
> At this point, we've got 19 marks for pretty straightforward analysis of argument. The watchword for getting these 19 marks, as for any analysis questions, is *accuracy*. You're largely stating what's there, so be careful that you don't lose these marks by being inaccurate (which includes being incomplete).
>
> Another analysis question in which accuracy is king is one that asks you to state an assumption. Let's do one next. The numbering of questions from 3 to 5 can vary, but the type of questions should be similar to what follows.

# Question 3

**(a) State one assumption that is needed for the conclusion in Document 2, paragraph 1 that 'zoos improve the welfare of animals compared to their lives in the wild'.**

All zoo enclosures are well designed.

All zoos employ highly skilled and imaginative staff.

All zoos provide enhanced environments for their animals.

The welfare of wild animals consists only in minimising or eliminating attacks by predators, starvation, disease, parasites, cold and heat.

> All these are necessary assumptions and would get the 3 marks. (You will have noticed that the hypothetical reasoning we looked at earlier required that the 'if' part of it *was actually the case*. This is always worth looking out for. When an author moves from a hypothetical reason to a conclusion that isn't hypothetical, he or she must assume that the 'if' part of the 'if…then' is the case. This gives us both the second and the third of the above statements.)

> To get the full 3 marks you need to have identified an assumption and to have expressed it carefully (indeed, not just carefully but exactly). So how does an examiner allocate the 2, 1 and 0 marks?

> Two marks would be awarded for less accurate statements:

All zoos are well designed.

> The 1-mark category is an odd one. It's as if it's been designed to accommodate people who phrase assumptions in a way that attacks what the author is saying. As you know, finding assumptions isn't a question of evaluation — it's not asking you to say whether or not the author is right to believe something. But this is what some people do, so the 1-mark place has been created for them:

Just because some zoos provide well designed enclosures doesn't mean that all do.

> This means that effectively you get a mark for straightforwardly being wrong!

> Given that a mark is given for being wrong, what on earth do you have to do to get 0? The mark scheme tells the examiner to give 0 'for the statement of an incorrect assumption' (having already told them to give 1 — or even 2 — for incorrect assumptions). So let's have a go at being even more incorrect. One obvious way would be to write something that's already stated by the author:

The daily lives of zoo animals can be enriched by the provision of enhanced environments.

> Another way would be to seriously misinterpret what the author is saying:

Animals in zoos can't be compared with those in the wild.

There is one more analysis-type question. It's different from the others that we've been looking at, in that it isn't asking you to identify or state something that's there (or, with assumptions, something that's there but you can't see it). This question asks you to continue the author's argument by adding a further reason.

**(b) Suggest one reason, other than those already given in Document 1, that could be used in an argument against zoos.**

Again, the examiner has four possible marks to award: 3, 2, 1 and 0. Here's an answer that should get 3 marks:

Zoos very often obtain their animals by having them stolen from the wild.

This satisfies the requirement of giving what is called 'clear support' to the argument. It provides a new line of reasoning and supports the conclusion well.

Here are two more examples which do the same:

In the name of entertainment and to attract visitors, zoos create cross-bred creatures (such as the zedonk, created from a zebra and a donkey).

Animals are often transported in very poor conditions over perhaps thousands of miles to zoos.

Two marks are given for reasons that provide 'limited' rather than 'clear' support to the argument. This involves the examiner having to make a judgement between limited and clear relevance. The next answer is an example of one which should fit this distinction:

Zoos make people forget that different animals live in different habitats.

This is the case. As we wander from tiger to camel, from llama to kangaroo, we forget that we're crossing continents. It's perhaps relevant to the problem of keeping animals in zoos but would need some development for its relevance to be clear.

The 1-mark answers are an assortment of types. These range from one extreme to another: from giving an argument rather than a reason, to giving information rather than a reason. There is a further example, which is to simply make a relevant point without expressing it in the form of a reason ('animal rights').

The 0, as usual, comes in via the door of irrelevance:

There are hundreds of zoos in the country.

We've now done the analysis questions and picked up 25 marks. Next we'll look at typical evaluation questions. You'll remember that when we looked at the evaluation skills you're meant to have, we focused first on the evaluation of statistical evidence. So this is where we start with our first evaluation question.

# Question 4

**Paragraph 3 of Document 2 gives the example of the African black rhino to support the claim that some species have to be managed (including taking some animals into captivity) in order to survive. Explain two ways in which this animal might or might not be representative of zoo animals.**

> Here you can see that we're looking at whether this example can be generalised to other animals. You could do this in different ways: two points showing that they're representative, two that they're not, or one each way. The examiner has 2 marks to give for each evaluation (explanation). Let's look at some that should give you 2 marks each:

The African black rhino could be very unusual because it's so endangered, so it's nothing like animals such as penguins and kangaroos.

The African black rhino could be very unusual because (unlike polar bears) it can be looked after satisfactorily in captivity.

The African black rhino might be typical of animals that are at particular risk of poaching and so managing them (including having them in zoos) is the only solution to ensure their survival.

> As you can see, we have provided what the examiner is hoping to find: 'clear explanation' of why the rhino is representative or not.

> The 1-mark score is given for what is termed 'unclear or limited explanation'. 'Unclear' here means the same as 'limited', which in turn means 'less than well developed'.

Black rhinos are typical of the problem of helping large animals.

> This is insufficiently developed in that it doesn't show why rhinos are typical. You can see, then, that because you're asked to 'explain' your evaluation, you need to show why your point is significant. If we look again at our first answer above, we can see how this is done.

The African black rhino could be very unusual *because it's so endangered, so it's nothing like animals such as penguins and kangaroos.*

> We've now got 4 more marks, giving us a total so far of 29.

> An alternative type of question in this part of the paper could refer you to an image presented as part of a document. This image will have a caption to accompany it, and the caption will be the focus of the question.

> For example, let's say that Document 3 included a photograph of a lion shown behind the bars of a zoo enclosure. The caption beneath it reads: 'Lions need space to roam.'

> The question on the significance of this caption could be something like one or both of these:

**Explain one way in which the photograph of the lion might give support to the caption.**

**Explain one way in which the photograph of the lion might give only limited support to the caption.**

An appropriate answer to the first would be:

The photograph emphasises the problem that zoos force lions to live in a way that is completely unnatural, since they are very restricted and unable to roam freely.

An unfocused answer to this first question would be:

The lion is in a cage.

An appropriate answer to the second would be:

The photograph shows only a lion behind bars. It doesn't show how much space the lion has to roam — the enclosure might be very large, enabling the lion to roam quite a long way.

An overly vague answer to the second question would be:

We don't know enough about the lion.

# Question 5

The final question in Section A is another one on evaluation. It could deliver a further 6 marks. You are now being asked to evaluate an argument in terms of assessing the significance of the reasons for the conclusion. It's more of an 'over to you' than most of the questions in Section A, in the sense that you could come up with quite a few different things. The marks are given in bands.
- You're asked to give an evaluation of two points of reasoning.
- Each point of evaluation must assess the relationship between a reason and the conclusion.
- Each point of evaluation should be 'detailed, accurate and well expressed'.

An evaluation which is 'detailed, accurate and well expressed' will gain you 5–6 marks, and one which is 'reasonably expressed' will get 3–4 marks.

**Consider the argument in Document 1 against zoos. Assess how far the reasons support its conclusion. You should include two developed points that refer directly to the links between the reasons and the conclusion.**

Even if 'the main purpose of zoos is to make money for their owners', this doesn't mean that 'zoos should not be seen as being concerned with the interests of animals'. By trying to make money, zoo owners will have to make their zoos appealing. This will involve ensuring that their animals are well cared for and housed in attractive enclosures, otherwise people won't want to come and visit a zoo.

If zoo animals 'often lead highly stressful lives', then this could certainly support the conclusion that zoos don't exist for the benefit of the animals in them. We would, however, need to know how often and why their lives are highly stressed. It could well be that the stress is due to normal aspects of an animal's life, such as the need to defend territory. The example that's given of elephants normally covering 30 miles per day in the wild might not be as relevant as the author thinks. Just because they do this in the wild, it doesn't mean that they suffer by not being able to in a zoo. (After all, years ago, people often used to walk much further than they do today.)

> That has to give us 6 marks. We've given two points of reasoning, each of which assesses the relationship between a reason and the conclusion. And each point of evaluation is detailed (lots of development, as you can see), accurate and well expressed.

> So what might 3–4 marks look like?

> You could get 4 marks by giving just one of these detailed, accurate and well expressed points. Or you could get this lower band mark by producing less well focused and only 'reasonably expressed' evaluations.

Captive breeding programmes could still be good because they could help to keep species like rhinos going. So making money for zoo owners is OK if rhinos survive.

> In this point of evaluation, as you can see, there is much less development (and so much less detail). In addition, the focus on the link between the reason ('the main purpose of zoos is to make money for their owners') and the conclusion is not made explicit.

> To get no marks at all, you would need to produce something that shows no evaluation of the link between a reason and the conclusion. For example:

It's very difficult to know if an animal is suffering stress. If they are, how does it show itself? People can be stressed and we wouldn't know just by looking at them. So looking at a giraffe or a zebra isn't going to tell us anything about whether they're stressed or not.

> In this answer, a problem with the reason is raised. It might well be an important problem (for example, smiling chimpanzees are stressed chimpanzees), but the answer needs to be focused on the implication of this problem for the relationship between the reason and the conclusion.

> So that's Section A completed. Thirty-five marks available. Thirty-five marks obtained.

The questions in Section B are all concerned with the problem of credibility. So in all of these you're required to apply the credibility criteria that we looked at earlier.

The first question is likely to ask you to evaluate the credibility of a report (which could well be one of the documents in the resource booklet). You'll need to show why you think particular criteria are relevant in assessing the credibility of the report.

# Question 6

**Assess how far the report described in Document 3 is credible.**

**You should make two points. Each point should identify and use a relevant credibility criterion to assess the credibility of the document, supported by reference to the text.**

There are 6 marks available here, 3 for each point that you make. You can see from the question what you have to do to get the marks:
- Identify a relevant credibility criterion.
- Apply it to the document.
- Refer to the document and/or its source.

Each of these tasks is worth 1 mark if correctly carried out. Do these twice and you can see that 6 marks are there for the taking. So let's see how this would work.

PETA's report could be seen as credible because it quotes from a study by 'scientists at Oxford University', a study which must be based on expertise because only scientists with considerable expertise would work at Oxford University.

You can see that we have done the three things that were asked for. Just to be sure, we'll show where we got the marks:

PETA's report could be seen as credible because it quotes from a study by 'scientists at Oxford University' *[1 mark for referring to the text]*, a study which must be based on expertise *[1 mark for identifying a relevant criterion]* because only scientists with considerable expertise would work at Oxford University *[1 mark for showing why the criterion is relevant]*.

We'll apply another criterion to get the other 3 marks.

PETA could be seen as having a vested interest in presenting information showing that zoos are a problem for the animal rights position *[1 mark for identifying a relevant criterion]* because it is 'the largest animal rights organisation in the world' *[1 mark for referring to the text]* and this would make it select only those studies that would support this position *[1 mark for showing why the criterion is relevant]*.

So we get the marks by doing these three things. It would follow that getting fewer than 3 marks will be the result of missing out at least one of these things.

PETA shows bias in the way it selects only that evidence which supports its position.

> In this answer there is no reference to the text, so the third mark cannot be given.

PETA must be biased because it refers only to a study by scientists at Oxford University.

> In this answer there is no useful explanation of why PETA is biased. Just because it refers to this study and no other study doesn't in itself show bias. You would need to show why referring to just this study is possible evidence of bias (that it fits with PETA's anti-zoo position).

> The next question uses the criteria of consistency and inconsistency. (It's really only one criterion, but in its positive and negative versions.) The question will give you a claim that's been made in one of the documents and ask you to find claims that are consistent and inconsistent with it. This should be pretty straightforward.

# Question 7

**The last sentence of Document 4 includes the claim that 'elephants should not be kept in zoos'.**

**(a) Identify a claim and its source in any of the other documents that would be consistent with this claim.**

As PETA says, elephants are one example of animals that 'become stressed and miserable in their restricted enclosures'.

> This will get the 2 marks. We have given both the claim (quoted) and the source. It is best to quote the claim, because the examiner will be able to match this with what they have in the mark scheme.

> Here's another 2-mark answer:

In Document 1 we are told that 'Even the apparently large enclosures sometimes provided for elephants cannot begin to provide the range of 30 miles per day that these animals normally cover'.

> Again both the source and the quoted claim are given.

> The 1-mark answer is for a claim without a source. (Giving a source without a claim leads, as you would expect, to 0 marks.)

> Although the claim that 'elephants kept in zoos die younger than in the wild' is consistent with the claim given in the question, it is from the same document, so would not be credited.

> The companion question to the one on consistency is, not surprisingly, one on inconsistency. We're going to change this a little by giving a different claim from the one used in 7(a). The way we answer the question is, however, the same.

In Document 3, PETA claims that 'although zoos claim to contribute to conservation, they actually take money away from useful conservation projects'.

**(b) Identify a claim and its source in any of the other documents that would be inconsistent with this claim.**

As before, two things are needed for the 2 marks.

BIAZA claims that many of its members 'specialise in conservation activities in areas where endangered species live'.

As before, we have given the two things that are needed for the 2 marks. We've given the source (BIAZA) and the relevant claim. It needs to be stressed that in both of the questions on consistency/inconsistency, you need to be very specific about the source of the claim. The claim in this last example comes from BIAZA, so this is what you need to write.

The usual move from 2 marks to 1 would follow if you gave a claim without a source. And, of course, the move to 0 would follow if your answer was incorrect.

BIAZA claims that zoos 'improve the welfare of animals compared to their lives in the wild'.

Though PETA and BIAZA disagree fundamentally with each other over whether or not zoos are a good thing, this claim by BIAZA is not inconsistent with the specific claim of PETA in the question.

You need to be careful about this. Just because sources are on different sides doesn't mean that any of their claims is inconsistent with any made by the other side. You need to match the consistency and the inconsistency closely to the specific claim given.

# Question 8

The next question returns us to the full range of credibility criteria that we started to use in question 6. It gives you some freedom in choosing which criteria to use in evaluating claims that are made. In fact, the freedom is twofold. You can choose not only which criteria you apply but also which claim.

The first, and main, part of the question has the following structure:

**Question 8 (a)**

**Assess the credibility of one claim made by X (in Document A) and one made by Y (in Document B).**

**Apply two credibility criteria to explain how these might strengthen or weaken the credibility of the claim.**

You can see the framework for what you have to do, and thus how the marks are going to be awarded.

Claim — 1 mark

Credibility criterion identified — 1 mark

Credibility criterion applied — 1 mark

Judgement of whether criterion strengthens or weakens claim — 1 mark

These 3 marks using credibility criteria are available twice in that you're asked to apply two criteria. It's nice when the marks are laid out so clearly and you can see exactly where they're being awarded.

So now we're clear about the task in this question, let's see how the framework of marks applies in practice.

**8 (a) Assess the credibility of one claim made by BIAZA.**

**Apply two credibility criteria to explain how these might strengthen or weaken the credibility of the claim.**

Here's our answer:

Claim: Zoos 'meet the needs of the animals in their care by understanding what constitutes good welfare, and by providing appropriate housing and husbandry'.

As the organisation that represents zoos in Britain and Ireland, it would have the ability to perceive what's happening on a day-to-day basis in zoos in order to form a judgement as to whether or not the welfare of the animals was ensured. This would therefore strengthen the credibility of this claim.

Before we give a second criterion, let's look at how the marks will be awarded for this answer.

Claim: Zoos 'meet the needs of the animals in their care by understanding what constitutes good welfare, and by providing appropriate housing and husbandry'. *[1 mark for correct identification of a claim]*

As the organisation that represents zoos in Britain and Ireland, it would have the ability to perceive *[1 mark for correct identification of a relevant credibility criterion]* what's happening on a day-to-day basis in zoos in order to form a judgement as to whether or not the welfare of the animals was ensured. *[1 mark for correct application of the criterion]* This would therefore strengthen the credibility of this claim. *[1 mark for identifying the effect of this criterion on the credibility of the claim]*

We'll apply another credibility criterion to get a further 3 marks.

As the organisation that represents zoos in Britain and Ireland, it would have the expertise needed to understand what is involved in meeting the welfare needs of zoo animals, in that its members have considerable experience of working with such animals. This would therefore strengthen the credibility of the claim.

Having produced two criteria which strengthen the claim, let's look at one to weaken it. (You can use any combination of strengthening and weakening in your choice of criteria. You could even use the same criterion for both — we'll look at an example of this below.)

As the organisation that represents zoos in Britain and Ireland, it would have a vested interest in presenting zoos in a good light by claiming that the animals in zoos are well looked after. (If people thought they weren't, they would be less likely to visit, thus reducing profits.) In this way, we can see that vested interest weakens the credibility of this claim.

In this last answer, we've spelled out the possible vested interest in enough detail for the examiner to be sure that we have shown that it is relevant here. It's always best to keep them happy!

We'll now look at a different claim. The question in the exam paper is likely to ask you to assess two different claims.

**Assess the credibility of one claim made by PETA.**

**Apply two credibility criteria to explain how these might strengthen or weaken the credibility of the claim.**

Here's our answer:

Claim: PETA 'has discovered that the Dickerson Park Zoo in the USA sold or "donated" a giraffe, a kudu, five kangaroos and two deer to Buddy Jordan, an "animal dealer who sells animals to exotic-animal auctions and breeders, unaccredited zoos, and even hunting ranches"'.

As the largest animal rights organisation in the world, PETA will have expertise in researching and understanding information about animal welfare. This means that it will be able to find out what is going on in zoos, including any sale of zoo animals. As a result, the credibility of this claim would be strengthened.

Let's just mark this before we move on to check that we're still doing what's needed. The claim has been accurately given, so that's 1 mark straightaway. Now we'll check the application of the credibility criterion:

As the largest animal rights organisation in the world, PETA will have expertise in researching and understanding information about animal welfare. [1] This means that it will be able to find out what is going on in zoos, including any sale of zoo animals. [1] As a result, the credibility of this claim would be strengthened. [1]

And now a criterion to weaken the claim:

As the largest animal rights organisation in the world, PETA will have a vested interest in showing zoos in a bad light. This means that it is likely to present a very selective picture of what goes on in zoos. As a result, the credibility of the claim is weakened.

We noted earlier that you can use the same criterion in two different ways, with two different outcomes. Here's an example of how this can be done:

As the largest animal rights organisation in the world, PETA will have a vested interest in presenting correct information so that it will be taken seriously by its supporters and those it wants to influence. As a result, the credibility of its claim is strengthened.

> Having looked at many examples of full-mark answers, let's just remind ourselves what lesser answers look like. This isn't difficult to do, because we know that lesser answers are going to miss out one of the things the question asks for. (Of course, you might be wondering what would happen if you gave an incorrect claim. Would that mean that all your carefully worded assessment would count for nothing? Fortunately not. Examiners are instructed to mark your answers in terms of how competent they are as assessments of this incorrect claim.)

> Here's an answer:

PETA will be biased in its reporting of Dickerson Park Zoo and Buddy Jordan, so its claim is weakened.

> In this last example, there is no explanation of why PETA will be biased, so a mark is lost.

PETA will be biased in its reporting of Dickerson Park Zoo and Buddy Jordan because, being the biggest animal rights organisation, it will want to select only that evidence that looks bad for zoos.

> In this answer, all the work has been done except to say why the bias (which has been explained) will weaken the claim. It might be irritating that you've got to spell it out in this way, because it's pretty obvious that the last answer is showing why the claim is weakened. But irritating or not, you've got to give the examiner all they want to get all the marks.

> We'll now move on to look at 8 (b).

> This question is asking you to look again at an assessment you have made in 8 (a) and to consider how you could make this assessment stronger by having more information. It is often the case that we judge the credibility of claims even though our information is inadequate. For example, we might take it that a source had the ability to perceive. But did they have sufficient access to be able to do this fully or accurately?

**Question 8 (b)**

**Explain what other information you would need to know in order to reach one of your points of assessment in 8 (a) about the credibility of *X*'s claim. You should make one precise point.**

> The wording of the question is not entirely helpful. What it means is, 'What other information do you need to have in order to make your assessment of the claim stronger?' That's how it needs to be interpreted, otherwise it doesn't make much sense.

> So let's have another look at two of our assessments that we did in 8 (a). Here's the first:

As the organisation that represents zoos in Britain and Ireland, it would have the expertise needed to understand what is involved in meeting the welfare needs of zoo animals, in that its members have considerable experience of working with such animals. This would therefore strengthen the credibility of the claim.

> Remember that the question the examiner is effectively asking you is, 'What further information do you need in order to make your assessment stronger?' You already know some things about BIAZA, and there were enough to make some assessment of any claim it makes. But what else would it be useful to know?

You would need to know whether the claim was based on information that BIAZA got from the staff who actually work day-to-day with the animals, rather than just from the owners and senior managers who might have little to do with the animals.

> In this answer, we've done two things. We've not only said what other information we need but we've explained why we need to have it. Three marks are awarded for an accurate and well developed answer.

> Here's another of our assessments:

As the largest animal rights organisation in the world, PETA will have a vested interest in showing zoos in a bad light. This means that it is likely to present a very selective picture of what goes on in zoos. As a result, the credibility of its claim is weakened.

> What else do we need to know to make this assessment stronger?

We need to know whether the sale or 'donation' of animals by Dickerson Park Zoo to Buddy Jordan was such an unusual example that it wasn't in any way typical of how zoos operate.

> In this answer we have focused on the need to know whether PETA was being over-selective in its use of evidence. If we had this information, then our assessment that PETA's claim was weakened would itself be strengthened.

> What do we need to do to get fewer than the 3 marks available? Here's a way of getting only two of them. First, here's the original assessment again:

As the largest animal rights organisation in the world, PETA will have a vested interest in showing zoos in a bad light. This will mean that it is likely to present a very selective picture of what goes on in zoos. As a result, the credibility of the claim is weakened.

> Here's our answer:

We would need to know if PETA has a vested interest in showing zoos in a bad light. We need to know this in order to help us to see if the claim is weakened.

> In this answer, we're not really getting anywhere. We're just asking for information on something that we've already stated is the case. We need information to strengthen this. Perhaps the wording of the question might lead you to answer like this. But don't be tempted to.

> And for just 1 mark?

You might answer this question by explaining why we need more information to assess the claim that's made. In other words, you are doing some assessment of the claim itself rather than of one of your assessments of it.

We need to know how BIAZA defines 'good welfare', because it might be using the term to include just physical health and so excluding mental well-being.

This is a good point! But unfortunately it isn't an answer to the specific requirements of this question. You need to remember to focus your answer on one of your assessments given in the previous question.

# Question 9

We're ready now to tackle the final question. It will ask you to look at both sides of the dispute and compare them in terms of their credibility and their plausibility (understood as 'reasonableness'). In the end, you'll need to make a decision as to which side is the more credible and plausible.

It's worth just thinking for a minute about the relationship between credibility and plausibility. Although they're two separate things, they are linked in an important way. For something to be plausible, it has to be credible, and vice versa. Did something happen? Is this likely or reasonable? The answers to these questions are very much to do with how credible it is that something happened or that something is the case. Similarly, is it plausible to believe one version or case rather than another? The answer to this question depends in part on how credible are those who are putting the version or case forward.

The final question is one of those where you're told what to do in general terms and then sent off to do it. There's none of the kindly leading by the hand that we've had in some earlier questions.

Given that our documents have been on the subject of zoos, our version of the question will reflect this.

**Referring to the material within the documents, come to a reasoned judgement as to whether zoos increase or reduce animal welfare. You should make a reasoned case with a judgement based on**
  - **the relative credibility of both sides**
  - **the relative plausibility of both positions**

Before we start to write an answer, it would be a very good idea to be clear about what we need to do.

What amounts to the same thing is actually given twice, although it's put slightly differently in the two versions. We need to produce 'a reasoned case with a judgement' and we need to 'come to a reasoned judgement'. It's strange that after all the work you've done on the nature of arguments, the word 'argument' isn't used here. It's strange because that's all you're being asked to do. (As you know, an argument is a 'reasoned case' that has to contain a judgement or a 'conclusion'.) So let's get to the point. *This question is asking you to write an argument.*

The next thing to consider is what sort of framework for the argument is being asked for? There are four points to remember here.

First, you need to make sure that you use the material in the documents. This isn't an opportunity for you just to write an argument on the subject in question. You'll get an opportunity to write an argument on a topic in the Unit F502 paper. What you're doing here is writing an argument based on the credibility and plausibility of the material that's given for each side. This involves you constantly referring to the material in the documents and assessing its credibility and plausibility.

Second, you need to explicitly use the credibility criteria by name in assessing the credibility of the material in the documents.

Third, you need to use your assessment of the credibility of the material in the documents in order to help you to assess how plausible is the case for each side. By this, you'll remember, we mean how reasonable is the case for each side.

Fourth, you will need to explicitly form a judgement in the way in which it is presented in the question. In this question we are asked to 'come to a reasoned judgement as to whether zoos increase or reduce animal welfare'. Thus your judgement couldn't be 'zoos are necessary' or 'zoos should be better controlled', because these don't fit with what's being asked. In our example, the judgement will have to be either 'zoos increase animal welfare' or 'zoos reduce animal welfare'.

There's an instruction that doesn't appear on the question paper but appears in the mark scheme, although it reads as if it's addressed to the candidate. Here it is:

**Your answer should include a sustained comparison within each of these tasks.**

So that is telling you that you need to be comparing both credibility and plausibility in a sustained way. We'll come back to this point when we've had a go at doing the question.

But before we start considering answers, let's have a look at what the examiner has in front of them when they're assessing your answer. They use a framework in which marks are awarded in bands, rather than for specific points that are made.

The top band marks are described as follows:

● The answer is detailed and accurate.

This shows that we need to include plenty of different points and to ensure that these refer accurately to the content of the documents, and that we make accurate use of the credibility criteria.

● The answer is well expressed.

There's a problem about what this might mean, but we'll aim to write an answer that's well organised and clearly expressed.

- The relative credibility of *each* side is assessed, so that a comparison can be drawn between the two sides.

This gives us part of the framework to use in putting our answer together. We'll need to show that we've used credibility criteria to examine the credibility of each side and then compare the two sides.

- The relative plausibility of *each* side is assessed, so that a comparison can be drawn between the two sides.

This gives us the other part of the framework to use in putting our answer together. We'll need to show that we've considered how reasonable each side of the case is in terms of the evidence provided.

- Effective reference to the documents is used.

We need to make sure that our points about credibility and plausibility are supported by relevant references to material in the documents.

There is, as usual, the reference to grammar, spelling and punctuation, but if your answer does all the things we've looked at it is unlikely to be marked down because of a few spelling and grammar errors.

It might have occurred to you that you could answer this question effectively by simply reproducing your answers to question 8 (a). You will remember that your answers to that question were assessments of the credibility of claims made by two of the sources. Well, don't think that you can simply reproduce your answers to that question and walk away. The examiner is told to be stern with such answers and to award 0 marks to those that simply reproduce what's been offered for 8 (a), without any further development.

Right, we now know what we've got to do to achieve the highest marks. So let's look at producing a top-grade answer. I know that you're itching to start putting words on the paper, to feel those marks stacking up in your account. But just hold back for a few more minutes.

What we need to do if we're to produce a well organised and effective argument is to go back to the documents and look for examples of the credibility criteria we're going to use.

- How do the examples compare in numbers? For example, does one side have more expertise than the other? Is one side heavier on the side of vested interest than the other?

- Are there examples of sources which have more than one positive credibility criterion (for example expertise + ability to perceive)? Are there examples of sources which have more than one negative criterion (vested interest + absence of ability to perceive)?

**section**

What about plausibility?

- Looking at the evidence on each side, which side produces the more reasonable case? How are the points raised by one side answered by the other? Does one side have evidence which makes its claim more likely to be the case? Are there any inconsistencies between the claims of one side? Has one side stacked up more relevant claims than the other?

This planning will pay for itself when you come to write your answer.

The case for zoos is represented by BIAZA and we can see that this organisation provides considerable relevant expertise in the area of zoos. This expertise could be at all sorts of levels. If you look at the members of BIAZA, these include what are described as 'world-famous zoos' such as London Zoo and Whipsnade, really big names in the zoo world. So the expertise of BIAZA is first of all in terms of the well established experience of its members.

But it's also in terms of the day-to-day experience. The zoos will be looking after thousands of animals, with possibly thousands of different species, every day. Their staff will include those who have specialist training in understanding these different species.

There's also the research side of BIAZA. It carries out a great deal of research, especially research into 'animal welfare', and this is published in the *International Zoo Yearbook* by the Zoological Society of London, a very important organisation with a wealth of knowledge and experience in understanding animals (and a high reputation for scientific work).

However, on the other side of the argument, we also have expertise. The organisation PETA is very big and will have accumulated a lot of knowledge and experience in understanding the issue of animal welfare generally. This expertise must then include welfare issues of zoo animals. In addition, PETA is able to refer to 'research carried out by scientists at Oxford University which showed that animals suffered in zoos'. This research must have been based on considerable expertise, given that it was carried out by scientists at one of the most important universities in the UK (and the world), with a high reputation for research.

The anti-zoo side has further expertise in the form of research published in 'the highly respected journal *Science*'. This journal must publish only material produced by people with relevant expertise.

We could also look for vested interest in the two sides. BIAZA will have a clear vested interest in getting people to believe that animals in zoos do not suffer. This vested interest comes from needing to show zoos in a positive light in order to continue to attract visitors, because without visitors there's no money. However, PETA could also be seen as having a vested interest in presenting only information that is anti-zoo. Given that PETA is an important animal rights organisation, its campaign would be weakened if it reported studies showing contented animals in zoos. Against this is another point. PETA's campaign against zoos is only one of many campaigns that it runs. So it is unlikely to have a vested interest here. BIAZA's vested interest is to report good things about zoos in order to survive. PETA will survive without the zoo issue. In addition neither the Oxford University study nor the one published in *Science* can be shown to be based on any vested interest that would benefit from reporting an anti-zoo position.

It can be seen that BIAZA's case is weakened by a clear vested interest in presenting a pro-zoo policy. The anti-zoo case is less weakened by vested interest, with even PETA not necessarily having a problem here.

The criterion of the ability to perceive is relevant to both sides. By working with zoo animals on a day-to-day basis, BIAZA will be able to see how zoo animals deal with the problems of confinement. PETA might have some ability to perceive, but this must be at a lower level than that of BIAZA. However, the research published in *Science* was based on more than 4,500 elephants both in the wild and in zoos. In addition, the Oxford study must have been carried out by the scientists looking at animals in zoos.

On balance, then, because of the vested interest issue, the credibility of the anti-zoo sources is stronger than that of the pro-zoo source.

So how plausible are the two cases? The pro-zoo case has two important parts. There is the point that animals in the wild suffer from various problems such as predators and disease, whereas zoo animals are protected, well fed, and given medical care. The other point is that there are issues of conservation which zoos can address. The example of the African black rhino is given. Both of these points are directly challenged by the anti-zoo side. Research is quoted showing that although zoo animals might not be at risk of predators etc., they suffer in different ways. Indeed research on elephants showed that life in a zoo had negative consequences for them, as reflected by their shorter life expectancy. A further challenge to the pro-zoo argument is that there is evidence of a zoo passing some of its animals to someone who is unlikely to care for them properly. (Having said that, this is not evidence against BIAZA, because it refers to an example from the USA.)

On balance, the anti-zoo case is not only rather more credible but is also more plausible. It is therefore more plausible that zoos reduce rather than increase animal welfare.

> So that's it. We've done everything that's been asked for. We've compared both credibility and plausibility and have come to a specific judgement (in the form requested in the question).
>
> Let's just look back at what's written to see what we've done.
>
> We looked at expertise (and reputation on two occasions) (paragraphs 1–5 of our answer), vested interest (paragraphs 6 and 7), and ability to perceive (paragraph 8). Neutrality could have come in with the *Independent* and Oxford University and *Science*. In fact we could have mentioned them on the way through without having to have big sections on them. If you can do this without losing focus and taking up too much time, then do it.

We not only looked at these criteria but throughout we compared the two sides using them. We then came to a judgement as to which side, on balance, was the more credible (paragraph 9).

Then we looked at plausibility (paragraph 10), again comparing the two sides throughout. You'll notice that in this section we looked at the points that each side had made and assessed them in relation to each other. This is what is needed. It's a bit like a boxing match. One side hits out and the other side responds, and so it goes on until one side can be seen to have landed more punches and thus emerges as the winner (the more plausible).

Then we came to a judgement (final paragraph), making sure that the judgement was in the form asked for in the question.

Checking what we've done against our list of what was needed for a top-band mark, we can see that we've done everything.

- The answer is detailed and accurate.
- The answer is 'well-expressed'. (Notice how we organised our answer by including 'signposting' used in argument. This 'signposting' includes words like 'however', 'in addition', 'on balance' etc., and helps the reader to follow the way in which the argument progresses.)
- The relative credibility of *each* side is assessed, so that a comparison can be drawn between the two sides.
- The relative plausibility of *each* side is assessed, so that a comparison can be drawn between the two sides.
- Effective reference to the documents is used.

We can see that we've done all of these things, so top marks please, examiner.

But of course, we might not be able to do all these things. Let's say that, for whatever reason (time, frozen-up brain, exhaustion), we hadn't written paragraph 10, although we'd then given a judgement as to which side was the more plausible. Thus all we'd done was to assess the credibility of the two sides. In this case, we'd have received a maximum mark at the bottom of the second band. Similarly, of course, if we'd covered just plausibility and not credibility, we would be treated in the same way. So you need to cover both credibility and plausibility to access the higher marks.

What about the even lower marks? The following answer would fall into a lower band:

BIAZA is on the side of zoos because that's its job. It will want people to come to zoos to look at the animals and see that they're well looked after. PETA is against BIAZA because it wants to stop people going to zoos, because it thinks that they're not good for animals. So PETA uses evidence that shows that this is the case. Animals are stressed and miserable, according to this evidence. It comes from scientists at Oxford University, which is a very good university and makes the evidence strong. BIAZA also carries out research, and some of this must be good because it is published in the *International Zoo Yearbook*. One of the members of BIAZA is London Zoo, which is world-famous, so it must have a very good reputation. PETA must also have a very good reputation because it's the largest animal rights organisation in the world. The *Independent* is a paper that is neutral and the fact that it published the research showing that elephants suffer in zoos makes this a strong piece of evidence. The number of elephants studied is very big, which would make the research good because the zoologists must have had the ability to perceive them. The ability to perceive is also something that people who work in zoos will have.

Animals in zoos have better lives than those in the wild, according to BIAZA. On the other hand, there is lots of evidence which shows that they don't. They're stressed and miserable in their small enclosures. This is understandable because they don't naturally live enclosed by glass or bars. Some animals might need help to stop them from becoming extinct, like the African black rhino, but most animals in zoos aren't like that. Zoos are not good places for most animals.

> Though this answer covers quite a lot of ground, it suffers from a number of things. It reflects a scatter-gun approach in which various credibility criteria are thrown in but none is properly developed. As a result, the discussion suffers from a lack of organisation: more organisation would have helped it to do a better job of making comparisons between the two sides.

> The first credibility issue that's being discussed is that of vested interest, but the term itself isn't used. The vested interest of BIAZA is considered but isn't adequately spelt out. We can agree that 'it will want people to come to zoos to look at the animals and see they're well looked after'. But the point being made here is a little wide of the target. BIAZA argues that animals are well looked after. The credibility issue of vested interest comes in with the question 'Does this mean that the animals are indeed well looked after?'

> There is a useful reference to Oxford University making the 'evidence strong' because it is a 'good university'. The suggestion that BIAZA's research is also good 'because it is published in the *International Zoo Yearbook*' would have benefited from a little more development to support this point.

> There is good use of the criterion of reputation. This is used with both BIAZA and PETA and, in both cases, is supported by an explanation of the reputation.

> The use of the criterion of neutrality is less successful. We need some explanation of why the *Independent* is neutral — it isn't enough just to claim that it is. Furthermore, even if it is, that would not be enough to show that the research on elephants was 'a strong piece of evidence'. It might have reported the research because it is a good news item and so the newspaper had a vested interest in publishing it.

> The criterion of ability to perceive needs a fuller development in the way it is applied to the research on elephants. The fact that a large number of elephants were studied isn't really the point — it's the probability that the researchers worked by closely studying the actual elephants. Ability to perceive is also applied to 'people who work in zoos', but again, this needs development to make the point properly.

The answer does attempt a comparison between the credibility of the two sides, and this is to be commended. It is just not developed enough to make the higher marks. It reads as if the writer wanted to pack in as many of their list of criteria as possible, rather than giving sufficient thought to how they would fit here.

The second paragraph turns to plausibility. As with credibility, it is good that the answer does attempt a comparison between the two sides. It would have been better if it had more explicitly used material in the documents, and had developed its points further.

The judgement certainly follows the comparison of plausibility in that it is consistent with it. Unfortunately it hasn't been expressed as it should have been. It should have said, 'Zoos reduce rather than increase animal welfare.'

So that's it. The last answer written. The last piece of punctuation put correctly in place. That's another 13 marks added.

It's now just a question of waiting for the notification of your A grade. Well done!